...ve ...

in R E

Michael **KINCAID**

Hodder & Stoughton
LONDON SYDNEY AUCKLAND

ACKNOWLEDGEMENTS

I am grateful to a number of institutions and persons for their help in producing this book. To John Hull, editor of the British Journal of Religious Education, I express thanks for permission to use parts of my article on 'Curriculum Development in Religious Education: the Scottish Approach', from Volume 1, Number 1, Autumn 1985. Thanks are due to the Scottish Examination Board for permission to include questions from its 1989 and 1990 Standard Grade Trial Examinations, and extracts from its 'Arrangements' documents pertaining to Standard Grade and Short Courses; and to the Northern Examination Association for allowing publication of examination questions from its Syllabus A, Paper 3, 'Contemporary Issues in Christian Perspective' 1988. I am grateful for their comments to Bruce Wallace, Allan Hawke and Stuart Ritchie, who all interrupted their busy schedules to read parts of the original manuscript. I wish to thank also John Rudge of the Westhill RE Centre for bringing me up to date on matters relating to GCSE and the National Curriculum. Last but by no means least, I am grateful to the teachers who took part in the piloting of Standard Grade Religious Studies. Without their enthusiasm and commitment, which was a credit to their profession, I doubt if I would ever have been motivated to put pen to paper. I am happy to dedicate this book to them.

The publishers would like to thank the following for permission to reproduce material in this volume:
Oxford University Press for extracts from Karl Popper *Objective Knowledge*; International Thomson Publishing Services Ltd for the extract from Paul Hirst *Knowledge and the Curriculum*, and for the extracts from *The Collected World of C G Jung*; Harvard University Press for the extract from Jerome Bruner *The Process of Education*; Aberdeen University Press and Professor McPherson of the University of Edinburgh for the extract from Gow and McPherson *Tell Them from Me*; The Scottish Council for Research in Education for extracts from *Ways of Teaching*; Falmer Press Ltd for the extracts from *New Directions in Educational Psychology*; HMSO for the extract from *Learning and Teaching in Religious Education*; Octopus Publishing Group for the extracts from *Religious Education in Secondary Schools* and Sue Townsend *The Growing Pains of Adrian Mole.*.

British Library Cataloguing in Publication Data
Kincaid, Michael
Learning in RE
I. title
200.71

ISBN 0-340-55779-6

First published 1991
© Michael Kincaid

Printed for the educational publishing division of Hodder & Stoughton Ltd, Mill Road, Dunton Green, Sevenoaks Kent by Page Bros, Norwich.

CONTENTS

PREFACE

The introduction of new courses in religious studies presents teachers with a series of new challenges. Both GCSE in England and Standard Grade in Scotland extend learning, assessment and certification to all students who choose to study religion in the middle years of secondary education. Although the compulsory nature of the subject has meant that religious education was always intended for all students regardless of ability, much of the time has been spent discussing content and aims, rather than considering ways in which the needs of all students might be met within the classroom. What is required is not another approach to religious education dealing with content and aims, but a more comprehensive way of looking at the subject which takes into account principles of learning and teaching.

This is a book for teachers and student teachers. It has emerged partly from my experience of working with teachers during the imlementation of a new Standard Grade course in Religious Studies for 14-16 year olds. Before becoming operational throughout Scotland, the course was piloted in twenty one schools between 1987 and 1989. At several points I have made use of notes and recollections formed during that period. On occasions these consist of descriptions of good practice; at other times they describe difficulties we encountered with particular aspects of learning, teaching or assessment. The key principles of learning and teaching, however, set out in the Introduction and developed throughout the book, can be applied to all stages of primary and secondary religious education.

The book is concerned to present a pedagogical theory which can inform classroom practice and aid teachers in their task of improving learning for all students. Consequently it is concerned with such questions as: how can we improve learning in RE for all students: how can we use asessment to improve learning? can we help students to think critically about religious and moral issues? what teaching approaches are most appropriate in the study of religions? how can RE contribute to students' personal development? how do we go about planning courses and activities in religious studies?

INTRODUCTION

They were a very agreeable group of fifteen year olds most of whom would be taking a number of certificate examinations the following year. They came to me once a week for forty minutes. I tried to vary my approach and provide a variety of activities but it wasn't easy. I had only recently taken over as Head of Department and was still trying to build up resources. We were studying Hinduism and I had set them an assignment relating to the Hindu ideas of Karma and Samsara. They were to find out as much as they could about each of these concepts and explain the relationship between them. It was my intention to follow this up with a class discussion to reinforce and consolidate their understanding. Before I could call the class together to begin this second phase of the lesson, a student exclaimed,

"What I want to know, is what's all this got to do with us?"
The ensuing debate shattered my complacency and sparked off a series of attempts to bring my classroom practice more into line with my students' real concerns. They were evidently looking for something which I was clearly not supplying. Although they were learning about religion and about its significance for believers, their plea was for greater relevance, for a consideration of the ways in which religions might inform their understanding of themselves - what's it got to do with me? As Michael Grimmitt and later SCCORE expressed it, students want to learn 'from' religion as well as 'about' it.[1] My problem was 'how?'

The next few years were spent grappling with this question. Should the whole curriculum throughout the secondary stage consist of units designed to foster understanding of religion and units designed to foster understanding of themselves? Or should each unit consist of both emphases? If so, how should this integration be achieved? If students in late primary and early secondary enjoy collecting information about religions, was there not a case for including at this stage more units entirely devoted to understanding aspects of religions? Or were there important aspects of personal development at that stage which should not be ignored? In any case was all this concern about personal development really necessary? Was it not sufficient to develop in students an understanding of religion and its significance for believers? Was there any need to go further? I saw little sign that teachers of other subjects were attempting to help their students learn from the subject as well as about it. True, students might not see the personal relevance of religion immediately but this will surely come later in life.

To make matters worse I was not very sure what was meant by helping students to understand themselves. Learning about religion seemed fairly straightforward although, at its worst, could amount to little more than an amassing of facts with little understanding. It is not surprising that much, if not most religious education, has been concerned with learning about religion and about the human experiences which lie behind it. The accusation, often heard from church schools that non-denominational schools are mainly concerned with learning about religion while they were more concerned with the religious and personal development of young people, undoubtedly has some justification; although the preoccupation in some church schools with doctrinal content has often given that accusation a rather hollow ring. Learning from religion, on the other hand, seemed fraught with difficulties particularly at a time when religous education was trying desparately to avoid any suspicion of indoctrination.

Throughout the seventies and early eighties I do not think teachers had the tools, nor was the educational atmosphere conducive towards making a success of learning from religion. The importance of students learning to evaluate, so essential if they are to reflect on their own beliefs and values and learn from other faiths, was not sufficiently recognised. The concern with personal development, although part of the thinking within religious education, was not nearly such a pervasive force in the curriculum as it is now. Moreover, the move towards teaching world religions, providing as it did a much expanded content base, meant that a concentration on facts and information was more rather than less likely.

Nor was sufficient emphasis given to the notion of learning for all. The nature of public examinations with their stress on providing courses suitable for only a small percentage of students meant that teachers' expertise was focussed on satisfying the aims of these examinations, which in the main did not include any explicit reference to developing students' understanding of themselves. Indeed, reference to personal understanding was frequently excluded within public examinations as something which belonged only within religious education. Religious Studies, on the other hand, the term most often used to descibe the study of religion within such examinations, was said to emphasise the academic study of religions; the focus here being on the breadth and depth of study undertaken. It was usually acknowledged, however, that this distinction was by no means an absolute one, and that elements of personal development might well form part of the teaching within religious studies but would not be formally assessed. With the advent of examination courses designed to cater for students of all abilities, and the introduction of short courses in Scotland, for example, which can be used to supplant school-based general religious education, this distinction now has little to commend it.

While working with teachers on the implementation of the new Standard Grade course in Religious Studies, I became convinced of the need for a 'pedagogy'; that is, a theory of learning and teaching which could combine ideas about curriculum with aspects of methodology and classroom organisation. In my own teaching I had been too concerned with questions about the nature of RE, with content and with aims. I began to realise that if we were to improve the learning and motivation of all students, some overall approach to learning and teaching was required, rather than simply the application of a particular theory of religious education. Implicit in students' desire for relevance was, I believed, a desire to be convinced not so much that religion mattered, but that 'they' mattered. All students needed to experience success at regular intervals and to feel that 'their' ideas and opinions counted. New examinations, with their emphasis on learning for all and on the teaching and assessing of skills, had introduced a fresh dimension. Much more attention would have to be given to enabling all students to achieve their full potential. Moreover, it soon became obvious that skills could not be taught by a presentation mode of teaching, characterised chiefly by the desire to convey information. Students had to learn by doing, by finding out things for themselves, by exploring ideas together and exchanging views on a range of issues.

Learning about religion requires attention to differentiation and to the fact that student's learning is rarely linear and often confused. Learning from religion requires attention to the structure with which information is presented, since this provides the initial framework within which students learn to reflect and make judgements. It also requires attention to the nature and development of evaluative skills through a commitment to learning by means of a range of discursive methods. However, as we become more confident that such measures are reaping real benefits in terms of students' learning we will be driven back, inevitably, to ask philosophical questions about the nature of the subject matter. Is the content of students' learning worthwhile or are there other more important areas of content in which they should be engaged? Philosophical considerations about the nature of religious education therefore cannot be ignored within any theory about learning and teaching.

There are, perhaps, four broad theories about the nature of religious education:

First, there is the 'catechetical' theory which emphasises Christian education and nurture in the faith. It sees the task of religious education as initiating children and young people into a religious heritage, passing on religious and moral values, and developing belief and commitment. This is the form traditionally found within the Christian Church but which has found its way into schools, either as a logical extension of Christian nurture, as in Roman

Catholicism, or simply because of the high value the Church has always attached to education generally, as in the Church of England. Increasingly though, a distinction is being made between the place of religious education and the role of the school as a whole. The implication is that whatever the school as a whole does to further Christian nurture in a wider context, this should be in addition to what is done in religious education.

The second theory is based on the assumption that religion is a significant area of human experience which deserves to be studied by all who wish to call themselves educated. Religions and quasi-religions represent an objective body of beliefs, values and practices which can form the basis of religious education programmes for all ages. Through systematic and progressive teaching students can be initiated into religion as a form of knowledge or mode of human experience, and helped to understand religions in a spirit of genuine openness to all faiths. It is this theory which dominates in the so-called thematic approach to the teaching of religion, with themes such as signs and symbols, festivals, pilgrimages and worship.

The third theory is the one described by the Schools Council Working Paper 36, although that document is sometimes mistakenly quoted as exemplifying the phenomenological theory described above. The Working Paper stated that religious education should include both a study of religious phenomena and a concern for personal relevance:

"We incline to the view that religious education must include both the search for meaning and the objective study of the phenomena of religion. It should be both a dialogue with experience and a dialogue with living religions, so that one can interpret and reinforce the other."[2]

These two elements within religious education were referred to in the document as implicit and explicit religious education. Explicit RE is centered on religious beliefs, values and practices. Implicit RE focusses on those human experiences which all human beings share and which give rise to the fundamental questions of life with which religions deal; experiences, for example, connected with relationships, with growing up, and with the inevitability of suffering. Some have seen implicit RE as merely laying the foundations for, or developing the sensitivities for 'doing' religion. This can be a source of confusion for some teachers who wonder what connection there is between religion and specific human experiences, and whether it would not be better to concentrate on more explicit religious education. Topics such as myself, friends, family, helping, although part of implicit RE, may contribute little to students' religious understanding unless they include some exploration of the questions and implications which arise for the children themselves. It is this which **a fourth theory** attempts to ensure by emphasising the process of personal development as well as the content of implicit religious education. At the infant stage, for example, this will involve drawing, writing and talking in response to such questions as 'What do you think? How do you feel? What makes you happy? At later stages the process will concentrate on helping students to understand the insights of religions to fundamental issues within human life, and on relating these to their own growing sense of personal and social identity. By highlighting the processes involved, this theory can contribute to students' personal development in a number of ways, but particularly through the search for meaning and value in life.

It would be possible to apply aspects of an approach to learning and teaching to any of these theories of religious education and achieve significant increases in student motivation and learning. Whatever the nature and balance of content, students may be highly motivated, enjoy what they are doing and be learning a great deal. It will be clear from the following pages that my own preference lies in emphasising those processes within religious education which contribute to students' personal development. I believe that such a theory has the best chance of meeting the demand for personal relevance in the curriculum. However, I do not think that any theory of religious education is sufficient in itself. Even the demand for personal relevance cannot be met by a preoccupation with the question, 'What is RE?' It requires in addition a comprehensive approach to learning and teaching. It is with such an approach that I am concerned in the chapters which follow. It might be helpful to the reader if I set out the key principles of this approach in advance. These are:

• If learning is to be effective for all students, we need to implement a view of learning which sees students as possessing a set of abilities open to continuous improvement, rather than having a general ability which is fixed and unalterable.

• Since students come to new learning with different stocks of these abilities, their success or failure and subsequent motivation, depends on the use of a variety of teaching styles as well as differentiated treatment.

• If learning in RE is to be effective for all students it must be developed in a structured way. That structure should be recognisable and intelligible to students and not only to teachers.

• If learning in RE is to be relevant, it must be seen to be contributing to students' personal development over a number of elements, but particularly to their search for meaning and value.

• An important element in students' personal development is the ability to take decisions in the moral sphere. Religious education has a major role in delivering moral education in the curriculum.

• Personal development is essentially a process. Crucial to that process is the growing ability to evaluate. Specific measures need to be taken to help students learn to evaluate.

• Effective learning requires the setting of achievable targets linked to appropriate methods and resources. These should be brought together in a way that allows students to experience success at regular intervals.

• Students' learning is rarely linear and problem-free. There is a need for some form of teaching assessment which will take account of students' weaknesses and misunderstandings.

NOTES AND BIBLIOGRAPHY

1   Michael Grimmitt and Garth Read, *Teaching Christianity in RE, A Companion to the Two Photo Packs Christians Today*, Kevin Mayhew, 1977. SCCORE, Scottish Central Committee on Religious Education, Bulletin 2, 1981, para.1.3.

2   Schools Council, Working Paper 36, *Religious Education in Secondary Schools*, Methuen, 1971, p43.

1   RECENT DEVELOPMENTS

*Outlines developments in Religious Education in Scotland and explains
the relationship between these and similar developments in England. The
nature and role of grade criteria and attainment targets is discussed with
reference to GCSE, the National Curriculum and the Scottish Standard
Grade. The shift towards skills within recent developments is noted and
a number of reasons for it are given.*

CONTENT AND APPROACH

Three years before the publication of Working Paper 36 in 1971, the Millar
Committee was set up in Scotland by the Secretary of State "to review the
current practice of Scottish schools (other than Roman Catholic schools) with
regard to moral and religious education and to make recommendations for its
improvement."[1] It took the view that the place of moral and religious
education must be justified on educational grounds and consequently drew a
distinction between the role of the school and the role of the church and
home. It concluded that "religious education is no longer aimed at producing
assent to any particular set of propositions or commitment to one particular
faith."[2] Instead the aims of religious education were to be seen in terms of
helping young people towards maturity, in promoting self-understanding, in
developing good relationships with others. For Millar, "the aim of religious
education is essentially the same as that of education as a whole."[3] And for
this the Committee claimed there was "basic agreement" within much of the
evidence submitted to it.[4]

Among its many recommendations the Millar report suggested the bringing
together of a group at national level "to study and develop the curriculum in
religious education."[5] In November 1974 the Scottish Central Committee on
Religious Education (SCCORE) was born with responsibility for both
primary and secondary. It immediately set itself a formidable task. This was
to prepare a curricular framework which could be developed to meet the
varying needs of pupils in different parts of Scotland and in denominational
schools as well as in non-denominational schools. According to SCCORE
education deals with human growth and development. The educational
justification of religious education lies in its attempts to contribute to this
process of development especially the spiritual dimension.

The strength of this contribution results from students' growing understanding of religion as:

  (a) A distinctive domain of knowledge and a way of interpreting experience and substantiating values.

  (b) A distinctive framework which helps them to focus attention on fundamental questions and problems, and

  (c) A motivating force in creative work in the field of art, music and literature; in moral and civil law; and in social customs.[6]

Despite its success in justifying the inclusion of religious education in the curriculum, SCCORE had said little that was new and did not move the subject beyond the discussion initiated by the Schools Council in its Working Paper. Its significance, however, lay elsewhere.

The main concern of Scottish religious education in the seventies had been to justify the place of religion alongside other subjects. Religious education was not the only subject which found itself examining fundamental questions and personal issues. There was seen to be considerable overlap with programmes of social education, social subjects and English. The edges of the subject were blurred. It was difficult to see a clearly recognisable curriculum slot for religious education. Many argued that the concerns of religious education were indeed important but this did not require a separate subject in a timetable that was already overcrowded. For these reasons it was important for the subject to have "points of reference which distinguish religious education."[7] These were provided by SCCORE's distinctive features: Transcendence, Communication, Relationships, Response, and Meaning. They emerged from the nature of religion itself and according to SCCORE represented the most significant of those elements "common to the religions of mankind."[8] On the other hand the document provided little scope for pursuing the ideal of personal relevance, dealing as it did with only one side of the religious education equation.

Implicit/Explicit RE

SCCORE's second contribution to curriculum development, 'Curriculum Guidelines for Religious Education' (Bulletin 2) was published three years after the first in 1981. It emerged firmly from the debates which took place among teachers in the second half of the 1970's. The debate centred around the two approaches to religious education, the implicit/explicit or more frequently, the existential as against dimensional. Few in Scotland, however, saw the issue in such stark terms. Those who laid the emphasis on the dimensional side and insisted that attention must be given to the description of religious phenonemena, also wanted to ensure that this did not rule out the student asking his or her own questions of the material and making his or her own responses to it. Those who started by taking seriously students experiences wanted nevertheless to ensure that religions contributed to the fashioning of students' own ways of life. In the task of learning from religion it was essential, they said, to take account of the phenomenology of religion.

Significantly, the element of personal quest was given a new prominence. "A major concern of religious education is to assist the pupil's own search and all that is taught in religious education should contribute towards this."[9] The main contribution of the document is to present two sets of objectives classified under knowledge, understanding, and evaluation. The first set relates to religions and other stances for living, and the second set to the pupil's search for meaning, value and purpose in life. In an important statement SCCORE insists that "there should be a constant dialogue between these two sets of objectives. Though they are distinguishable, they cannot be separated in any worthwhile religious education."[10] At one level Bulletin 2 had carried the discussion forward considerably. It not only recognised the need for both elements within religious education but in its analysis showed what would be involved if teachers wanted to follow this through. With its analysis of the study of religion and the pupil's search, it did for both elements what 'Groundplan'[11] had done for one. At another level there now existed an even more urgent need to indicate how teachers could present religions phenomenologically, while at the same time assist students in their own search for meaning and value.

About the same time a number of local education authorities in England were preparing new syllabuses for religious education and similarly emphasising the importance of students learning from religions. It began in 1978 with the Hampshire syllabus which saw religious education as involving the personal quest for meaning and the search for values as well as the encounter with living faiths. "Many pupils", it observes, "are engaged in a personal search for meaning, purpose and values. A religious education which is seeking neither to indoctrinate nor to persuade should afford them positive help in the search."[12] This was followed in the early eighties by the Hertfordshire and Berkshire syllabuses.[13] In the former students were expected to "explore man's search for meaning and purpose... and relate this to their own search". While in the latter its title, 'Religious Heritage and Personal Quest' clearly speaks for itself.

One suggestion for bringing the implicit and the explicit together was proposed in a SCCORE working document in 1983.[14] It was to use the three concepts of meaning, value and purpose as the organising ideas in the curriculum. These key concepts were seen to include all aspects of the content of religious education since both religions and the student's search are forms of the human search for meaning, value and purpose in life. Another is contained in the report of the Working Party on Draft Grade Criteria for England and Wales.[15] It saw the idea of 'spirituality' as central to and distinctive of religion. Spirituality, says the report, can also provide a way of bridging the gap which has arisen between what appears to be two different ideologies of the subject, one placing the emphasis on the objective phenomena of religion, and the other arguing for relevance and the importance of experience. The Working Party was unhappy about any narrow interpretation of spirituality which restricted its meaning to a sense of God or Gods, much preferring a broader definition which made reference to "the purpose and meaning of life itself" or "matters at the heart and root of existence".[16]

At a more practical level SCCORE recommended that a religious education curriculum should contain two types of units. The first type is where the emphasis is on religions although the unit "should be developed in such a way as to relate the outward expressions of the religion to the ideas and experiences that lie behind them." The second type is where the emphasis is on the student's search although similarly the unit "should be developed in such a way as to draw upon the experience and insights of the great religions of the world."[17]

This seems to me very similar to what is contained within the Westhill Project. There the authors characterise the traditional approaches to religious education as the 'Systems' approach and the 'Life Themes' approach. The authors argue that teachers should be "quite clear about the purpose of each approach and about which one is being followed in any teaching situation."[18] They are rightly critical of the thematic approach to the teaching of religions. This approach attempts to organise learning on the basis of themes such as pilgrimages, festivals, signs and symbols, which are taken to be common to most religious traditions. "We suspect that this approach usually distorts the traditions and does little to develop children's understanding of the subject"[19] This is quite different, for example, from courses in the phenomenology of religion, which might be pursued by senior students in schools or students in university departments of religious studies. Here the object is to discover commonality with a view to saying something about religion in general as opposed to specific religions. The purpose of the Systems approach, say the authors, is to explore an aspect of a belief system in order to build up understanding of that system. Although the main emphasis within the Systems approach will be on one particular system, "the nature of the subject demands that links should be made with shared human experience and with the ideas and experiences of the children in the classroom." The purpose of the Life Themes approach is to explore an aspect of human experience in order to develop understanding of that experience and the ultimate questions it raises. Although the main emphasis within the Life Themes approach will be on an aspect of human experience, "the topic... will have potential for raising ultimate questions and for that reason there will be important links with the traditional belief systems."[20]

Recent Criticism

John Sealey has recently criticised approaches to religious education which want to include reference to the 'implicit' or which express a desire to contribute to students' personal development. He sees in this view an assumption that RE is in some way superior to or at least different from other subjects. He is sceptical about attempts to justify the subject in terms of some sort of social understanding or personal knowledge. He criticises Edwin Cox for implying that RE ought to have an impact on students different from other subjects in the curriculum. Subjects such as history or literature, he says, develop a student's understanding and ability to "evaluate the meaning of the field at a point one step removed from himself".[21] In his view it is sufficient to study religion for its own sake. There is no need to justify RE on any grounds "other than that of studying and understanding the nature of religious phenomena, including its claims to truth".[22]

It seems to me that education has failed if it does not go beyond developing understanding, if it does not also provide students with the ability to think for themselves. A religion's claim to truth consists of claims about human identity, relationships and ultimate meaning. I do not see how one can prevent students from considering different views about these. They will form judgements and make up their minds on religious and moral issues whether we like it or not. It is surely better that we organise students' learning so that they have the opportunity to discuss these issues as part of their education in religion. Otherwise religion will appear irrelevant to the great questions people face in real life. And more importantly, if education is restricted to understanding, students will be ill-equipped to perceive religion and religions as relevant to 'them', as a possible and legitimate interpretation of human experience. Nor am I sure how students are to evaluate the meaning of a field "at a point one step removed" from themselves. This obviously reflects a phenomenological model of religious education which advocates the temporary 'bracketing out' of the student's own beliefs, ideas and assumptions in order to enter imaginatively into the experience of religious believers. Except in the upper school I doubt whether students have sufficient intellectual or emotional maturity to achieve such objectivity. This is not only a problem in religious education. There is plenty of evidence in the teaching of science, for example, that students' inability to 'bracket out' their commonsense understanding of scientific concepts and processes, constitutes a real barrier to effective learning.[23]

If RE must avoid concern for personal development to bring it into line with other subjects, then where is such concern to find expression in the curriculum? Is it to be restricted to guidance and pastoral care? This would display a rather narrow understanding of the ways in which the curriculum can contribute to students' personal development. All subjects, to differing degrees, will have an influence on students' attitudes and values, intentionally or unintentionally. This influence may arise in relation to teacher/student relationships and classroom organisation, or through the content of courses which touch on aspects of, for example, tolerance, responsibility, equal opportunities and care of the environment. In forming judgements on these and other matters, albeit provisionally, students will be contributing to the growth of their own personal outlook on life. In religious education they will judge for themselves how far religious beliefs can make sense of their own experience and provide answers to their questions about meaning, value and purpose. Judgements may be made on the basis of a range of different criteria, philosophical, historical, psychological or moral. But they will also be based on the criterion of personal relevance. In practice, however, these criteria are not always easily distinguishable.[24]

THE SEARCH FOR CRITERIA

The Ordinary grade of the Scottish Certificate of Education for all subjects was introduced in 1962. The standard set for the examination was one in which pupils at the lower end of the top 30% of the ability range could be expected to pass in at least three subjects. Within a few years many more candidates were being presented for 'O' grade than had been originally intended. The lure of a national examination with the possibility of a nationally recognised qualification proved far too attractive to pupils, parents and teachers.

The trend towards increasing presentations was significantly boosted when in 1972 the Scottish Certificate of Education Examination Board as it was then called, announced that from the following year a system of banded awards would operate replacing the familiar pass/fail system which had existed in the 'O' grade hitherto. Bands were to be awarded on an A-E scale with bands A-C representing that range of marks for which candidates had previously gained a pass. Although the subsequent increase in presentations led to some corresponding increase in the numbers of those who gained awards it also meant that many others had very little chance of success. By 1976, 76% of pupils presented for one or two 'O' grades, and 40% of those presented for three or four 'O' grades, failed to gain a single award in the A-C bands.[25] Clearly many students were following courses which were proving beyond their abilities. This situation pointed to the need for an urgent review of the ordinary grade examination.

The problem of finding an appropriate examination at age 16 was closely linked to concerns about the curriculum. By the mid-seventies it was generally thought that the Scottish secondary school had not yet found a satisfactory solution to the problem of providing appropriate and relevant courses for those students thought to be outside even an extended 'O' grade system. Curricular materials and resources produced in response to the raising of the school leaving age had proved unpopular with teachers and "most of these schemes never reached the stage of widespread implementation in school classrooms."[26] It was felt that many students being entered for non-certificate courses were being offered a much narrower choice of subjects for study than was available to students on certificate courses. Moreover the lack of a clear target for non-certificate students in the form of a national examination was judged to be a major factor in their low motivation.

Many of the inadequacies of the prevailing assessment and examination system were revealed in a trenchant and hard-hitting survey of consumer opinion. In the book, 'Tell them from me' school leavers were allowed to speak for themselves and made the most of the opportunity. One of them explained: "I don't actually think that anyone should be able to say what I can do and can't do. When we were at the ... school we were told that we would be able to sit 2 'O' grades... But even though I passed the exams, the education didn't think that it was good enough to sit an 'O' grade, so I never got to. Actually it is a fact that not one person in my course got to sit an 'O' grade. That is the thing I didn't like, plus the fact after sitting exams in the last year we never even got a report card."[27]

With the intention of remedying just such a situation the Consultatative Committee on the Curriculum, which advised the Secretary of State in Scotland on all curricular matters, set up a committee of inquiry under the chairmanship of James Munn early in 1975. Its purpose was primarily to consider how the curriculum for 14-16 year olds should be structured in order to ensure that all students received a balanced education appropriate to their needs and abilities. It was published in 1977 under the title, 'The Structure of the Curriculum in the Third and Fourth years'. At the same time a second committee chaired by Joseph Dunning was appointed to inquire into assessment and certification arrangements. Its remit included the charge to "consider what form or forms of examination or assessment would be most likely to meet the needs of fourth year pupils of varying academic ability". Its report appeared in the same year under the title, 'Assessment for All'. Widespread reforms of both curriculum and assessment for 14-16 year olds were recommended by these two reports, and implementation of Standard Grade, as it was called, began in 1983.

The reasons for reform, unsuitable courses and examinations which left most pupils with records of failure, were essentially those which later led to GCSE in England. The solutions proposed in Scotland, however, were initially more far-reaching and more closely integrated than in the rest of Britain.

This was made possible by the fact that due mainly to its size, Scotland has traditionally displayed a more centralised education system than is seen south of the border. It has, for example, only one examination board. The central features of the new system included scope for teachers to carry out their own internal assessments. The assessment, both internal and external, was to lead to certification for all students, and the certification was to be based on grade related criteria. Most of these features also exist within GCSE although the arrangements for internal assessment and external certification differ considerably between the two systems.

GCSE and the Draft Grade Criteria

In GCSE, school-based assessment of coursework is a central component of overall assessment carrying variously between 20% and 40% of the total percentage marks available. The requirements for coursework also vary between examining groups. With the Northern Examining Association, for example, three 'mini' projects will be sufficient whereas with the London and East Anglia Group ten short assignments will be asked for. In Standard Grade religious studies internal assessment takes two distinct forms. Firstly, one assessment objective or element, 'Investigating' is assessed within the school by means of a project. Students are required to investigate an issue of belief or morality and prepare a report of between 500 and 1000 words. The element 'Investigating' carries a weighting of one third, as do the other two elements 'Knowledge and understanding' and 'Evaluating'. Secondly coursework must be assessed regularly in order to arrive at an accumulated grade for each of the latter two elements. These accumulated grades function as estimates of candidates' performance. They are subsequently compared with the actual grades achieved by candidates in the external examination before arriving at a final grade.

In GCSE religious studies differentiation within the external examinations is achieved by means of a common paper across the whole range of abilities. Questions are arranged in ascending order of difficulty so that less-able students can achieve some success in the early part, while the most able are likely to be successful in all parts. Candidates being presented for the Northern Examining Association have question papers divided into three parts, A,B and C. Part A consists of short answer questions, part B is made up of structured questions introduced for example by a picture stimulus, while part C requires candidates to write more extended answers. In Standard Grade differentiation is brought about through separate examination papers. Three levels of examination papers are offered, Foundation, General, and Credit, with Credit being the most difficult. Each level is further differentiated across two grades- Foundation covering grades 6 and 5, General, grades 4 and 3, and Credit, grades 2 and 1. Each candidate can take any two adjacent papers, that is, Foundation and General or General and Credit allowing candidates to achieve across any one of four grades.

Grade Related Criteria or Grade Criteria, are statements of what candidates have to achieve before they can be awarded a particular grade. They are descriptions of student performance or competence which attempt to set out in positive terms what students know, understand and can do. In England the Secondary Examinations Council took the decision to forge ahead with Grade Criteria early in 1984. It was some years later, however, before draft criteria were produced for religious studies. The Working Party which produced them pointed to the major emphasis on skills within GCSE and concluded rightly that "the introduction of Grade Criteria would mark a further significant step forward in this direction".[28] Within the cognitive area it identified three groups of skills or domains, Investigation, Analysis and Classification, Application and Evaluation. In addition to assessing the cognitive, the Working Party also thought it important to assess affective skills. Religion involves emotions and commitments and this, it was argued, should be reflected in the processes of assessment. It stated, "there must be opportunity for candidates to display their responses to activities that bring them into an encounter with religion".[29] The Working Party went on to identify another two groups of skills within the affective area, namely, Empathy and Self-understanding. Empathy is concerned with insight into the feelings and actions of others, while self-understanding is directed towards improving awareness of one's own thoughts and feelings.

Having identified these domains the authors of the report proceed to locate four levels of achievement appropriate to these domains. These are designated:

Level 1   'The Descriptive Level'
Level 2   'The Consolidation Level'
Level 3   'The Discernment Level'
Level 4   'The Autonomous Level'.

These levels appear not to be based on any perceived heirarchy of skills within each domain, but on some overall heirarchy more or less applicable to all the domains. It is this that results in a number of significant differences between the proposed criteria in GCSE religious studies and those operating within Standard Grade. For example, the criteria which are arranged under 'Evaluation' in Standard grade are to be found within 'Self-understanding' as well as 'Application and Evaluation' in GCSE; expressing and justifying a personal response, presenting a developed argument, and drawing conclusions.

Similarly, the criteria arranged within the element 'Understanding' in Standard Grade are to be found in the domains 'Analysis and Classification' as well as 'Application and Evaluation': explaining the meaning of concepts, analysing concepts in terms of differing interpretations and contexts, and explaining the inter-relationship of concepts. Although appropriate differences of complexity can be seen between the levels in the cognitive domains, this is not so obvious in the affective domains. It is not clear to me at any rate, why 'expressing one's own beliefs and values' belongs only at Level 2, or why 'formulating a personal response to the beliefs and values of others' belongs at Level 3. The use of five domains with four levels of achievement in each would have made the system of assessment extremely unwieldy and, as has already happened north of the border, would probably have required some simplification had they been put into operation. As it was, research into the use of grade criteria across a number of subjects concluded that they were largely unworkable and development was halted. Nevertheless, the analysis of domains and levels of performance within Religious Studies still has much to offer and deserves to be taken seriously.

The National Curriculum

For most subjects the advent of the National Curriculum and a national system of assessment for 5-16 means that attainment targets will have to form the basis of criteria for GCSE. The position of Religious Education in the National Curriculum, however, makes this much less certain. The Education Reform Act requires Core and Foundation subjects to set out Attainment Targets, Programmes of Study and Assessment Arrangements for each of four Key Stages - 4-7 years, 7-11 years, 11-14 years and 14-16 years. The Core subjects are English, maths and science and the majority of curriculum time at primary level is to be devoted to these three subjects. As far as religious education is concerned the Act says that Local Education Authorities must have a 'locally' Agreed Syllabus. Religious education therefore is not required by law to follow the same pattern as other subjects.

In a handbook for teachers, however, produced by The Regional RE Centre of Westhill College, an attempt is made to set out a scheme for attainment and assessment in RE using the broad framework layed down for the Core and Foundation Subjects of the National Curriculum.[30] Significantly, and wisely in my view, the Westhill group has not attempted to devise criteria across ten levels in order to fit in with the general pattern of the National Curriculum. Instead, Attainment Statements have been written for each of the four Key Stages. For all subjects it has been recommended that a number of 'Profile Components' be identified. These represent important areas of the subject, in terms of knowledge, understanding and skills, which seem worth assessing and reporting. In RE the Handbook suggests three components:

- Knowledge and understanding of religious belief and practice;
- Awareness of life-experiences and the questions they raise;
- Exploring and responding to religions and life-experiences and developing positive attitudes.

Each Profile Component is sub-divided into Attainment Targets. These represent in general terms, what all students throughout the four Key Stages should be aiming to attain. Altogether there are ten attainment targets distributed across the three components. Each target is related to a particular feature of religion or human experience. For example, one of the Attainment Targets for 'Knowledge and understanding of religious belief and practice' relates to 'Worship and Meditation'. The Attainment Target is: "Pupils should develop a knowledge of practices associated with worship and meditation, and an understanding of the concept of worship as expressing an attitude to life focussed on God or on a spiritual goal."

The features of religion and human experience for which an Attainment Target is described, are as follows:

Key Stages 1-4

Profile Components	Knowledge and understanding of religion	Awareness of Life-experiences	Exploring and Responding
Features of Religion and Human Experience	Worship and Meditation Celebration Lifestyle Authority Belief and Identity	Natural World Relationships Ultimate Questions Expressing Meaning	Exploring and Responding

For each Attainment Target there are a number of Attainment Statements within each Key Stage. These describe how students, within each of the four Key Stages, will demonstrate their attainment of each target. In other words, expected student performances are described for ten targets at four levels of achievement. Most students will be expected to reach each level by age 7, 11, 14 and 16 years. For example at Key Stage 4, the Attainment Statements for the Attainment Target relating to 'Worship and Meditation' outlined above are: (a) show understanding of the symbolic nature of religious worship;
(b) understand the purposes of worship or meditation, and be able to use the concept of worship/meditation appropriately in describing the behavior of religious believers;
(c) be able to identify and explain features of places of religious significance which point to their sacredness;
(d) understand the concept of life as a pilgrimage[31]

Standard Grade and GRC

While the Secondary Examinations Council was announcing its decision to go ahead with Grade Criteria in 1984, Standard Grade courses and Grade Related Criteria were being introduced into Scottish schools in four subjects,

English, Mathematics, Science and Social and Vocational Skills. Pilot studies had already taken place in these subjects resulting in a substantial amount of criticism that assessment in Standard Grade courses was unduly complicated. Initially, Grade Criteria were defined for six grades and with most subjects supporting four or, in the case of Mathematics, five elements or domains, it is perhaps not surprising that teachers found the assessment procedures unnecessarily burdensome. In addition subject Working Parties had great difficulty in defining criteria at each of six grades and frequently produced statements which were complex and ambiguous. Consequently, when in 1986 assessment in Standard Grade was reviewed, it was recommended that subjects define criteria for only three levels, and that where possible the number of elements be reduced also. Two grades would be associated with each level so that reporting could continue to be based on six points of positive achievement.

Piloting in Religious Studies began in June 1987 in twenty-one schools throughout Scotland. At first teachers concentrated on the organisation of learning, introducing a range of approaches to facilitate both independent and cooperative learning. Although a number of problems arose concerning the interpretation and function of Grade Criteria, teachers had developed considerable familiarity with them by the end of the two years. This was nowhere more evident than in the internal assessment of'Investigating' when teachers demonstrated that they had developed the skill of applying Grade Criteria effectively to students' work. Throughout the pilot study Grade Criteria functioned mainly as assessment tools. They sometimes formed the basis of teachers' coursework assessments although teachers were advised that there was no need to grade every piece of work students completed. When Grade Criteria were first tried out in Scotland it led to a great deal of over-assessing or, to be more accurate, over-grading. The group which reviewed assessment therefore felt bound to offer the following advice:

> "We do not believe that... criteria should be used in a routine way to attempt to assign a grading to a pupil on the basis of a particular learning experience. Our view is that slavish application of grade related criteria to evaluation of each piece of work... is, at best, laborious and, at worst, distracting and potentially misleading."[32]

Grade Criteria were also used in the preparation of examination questions reflecting the criteria for different levels of achievement. We had to be able to look at any question and judge which criterion or criteria were being tested. In addition to their value as assessment tools, Grade Related Criteria are also important for teaching. They can first of all serve as a series of long term targets which teachers and students should be aiming to achieve over the course as a whole. These long term goals can then be used in short term planning as the source of learning outcomes for a particular sequence of lessons. Finally they act as a useful reminder that tasks and activities need to be varied sufficiently to allow students to achieve across the whole range of grades.

If we look briefly now at the following example of a GRC we can see that there is no attempt to create a statement which is so closely defined as to be unambiguous. This in any case would be difficult to achieve.

"The candidate can express a coherent opinion on an issue and support it with several valid reasons"

The obvious limitations of verbal descriptions means that there is always likely to be some degree of generality in any statement. For practical purposes all that is required is for definitions of performance to strike a balance between "woolly brevity and accurate verbosity".[33] Short, vague utterances are no guide to teaching and assessment. On the other hand the more accurate you want your definitions the more wordy you need to become, thus rendering the statements ultimately unmanageable. It is a mistake, therefore, to think of GRC as representing measurements of achievement in absolute terms. If this were the case then answers to questions would need to be either right or wrong, acceptable or unacceptable; the criteria are either met or they are not, with no room for partial credit and the exercise of professional judgement. This would be grossly unfair to many candidates and would hardly reflect the true nature of the subject.

FROM CONTENT TO SKILLS

"Thatcher Changes Course of History" read an Observer newspaper headline. It referred of course to the interim report of the national curriculum history working group for England and Wales. Mrs. Thatcher, it was reported, had instructed her new Education Secretary to take a tough line and insist on more British history, a more chronological approach and greater emphasis on facts rather than on skills. The supposed dichotomy between content and skills turned out to be a central and persistent feature of media coverage about history. This despite repeated statements by educationists that such a debate was false and sterile. As one member of the committee put it, "You can't argue whether Stalin was good or bad without knowing about the collectivisation of farms, pogroms and massacres."[34]

A concern to promote the development of skills as well as the learning of facts has been part and parcel of all recent educational change. Such a concern I would argue lies at the heart of the new GCSE and Standard Grade examinations. In November 1986 a colleague and I had the pleasure of attending a conference in Westhill College, Birmingham. At that conference Dr. John Rudge emphasised how learning was to be student-centred and based on a variety of activities. Teaching would focus more on the ways in which we acquire knowledge and understanding, and would involve encouraging students to respond personally through the development of the skill of evaluating. And he pointed out that within coursework the objectives are weighted away from knowledge towards the assessment of skills. In Standard Grade too, across all subjects, there has been an attempt to move away from covering content towards developing skills. It is hoped that reductions in content will benefit particularly the less able allowing them greater opportunities to cover a smaller volume of content while at the same time developing essential skills. One report states: "Thus there has been established as a fundamental principle of all Standard Grade courses that the quality of learning, the teaching process and the development of skills are more important than the quantity of factual content required for recall."[35]

So what lies behind this shift of emphasis and what are the implications for learning and teaching? There seem to be at least two sets of factors at work here:
1   Changing views about the nature of knowledge
2   Nature of learning and the learner

1. Changing views about the nature of knowledge

The Munn report, which initiated reform of the curriculum in Scotland, identified three sets of claims on the curriculum, from society, from the needs and interests of the learners, and from the nature of knowledge. It went on to discuss the nature of knowledge including the view that knowledge is divided into a number of forms or categories. Whether the differences between disciplines are mere conventions or whether there are good reasons for sub-dividing knowledge into such categories is a matter best left to the philosophers. Certainly there is no simple consensus on how many disciplines or forms of knowledge there actually are. In the literature answers range from 3 to about 8 categories. J.J.Schwab, for example, the American curriculum theorist, suggests that there are three kinds of disciplines - 'investigative', mathematics and the natural sciences; the 'appreciative disciplines', the Arts; and the 'decisive disciplines' the social sciences.[36] Another American, Philip Phenix, suggests that education is essentially about the search for meanings. He claims that there are six distinct but related 'realms'of meaning.[37]

- Symbolics: language and mathematics
- Empirics: the sciences of the physical world
- Aesthetics: the arts; eg. music, the visual arts and literature.
- Synnoetics: knowledge of ourselves and others
- Ethics: concerned with obligation and personal conduct
- Synoptics: history, philosophy and religion

The best known and most influential theory in this country is that of Paul Hirst. According to Hirst all knowledge can be differentiated into a number of 'logically distinct domains or forms'. These forms can be distinguished from each other in three ways. First, there are distinct kinds of concepts that characterise different types of knowledge; second, these key concepts are linked together in relationships which give the subject its particular structure; and third, the forms can be distinguished by different types of truth criteria. Hirst claims there are seven forms of knowledge:[38]

- mathematics and formal logic;
- the physical sciences;
- the human sciences including history;
- moral understanding;
- religion;
- philosophy;
- aesthetics.

While accepting much of Hirst's analysis, J.P.White develops the forms of knowledge into a curriculum sub-divided into what should be compulsory and what should be offered as optional experiences. His compulsory curriculum is roughly composed of three parts: the natural sciences, the social sciences and the humanities. In addition to these 'fundamental activities' the school curriculum should include the study of different ways of life, as well as opportunities to integrate these with students' own situation. And it is at this point, says White, that some kind of religious education becomes essential.[39]

Despite the evident diversity within the 'forms of knowledge' approach there is within it a common assumption regarding the objective nature of knowledge and truth. Knowledge exists largely independent of ourselves waiting to be discovered and learnt through familiarity with its different forms. It is through these 'forms' that we impose meaning and structure on our experience and therefore they should provide the organising principles of the curriculum. Thinking of the curriculum in this way, some have argued, is likely to give too much weight to the cognitive aspects of learning at the expense of the affective and practical aspects. Knowledge is too easily thought of as something 'out there' into which students must be initiated. Knowledge becomes something which is only found in books, and in the sacred writings and creeds of religions. This view of knowledge as objective, impersonal and unchanging is associated with the Rationalist and Empiricist traditions of philosophy but its roots are to be found as far back as the philosophy of Plato.

In the latter half of the twentieth century a growing body of work appeared offering a somewhat different view of knowledge and sharing a different set of assumptions. First, the person is not just a passive receiver of impersonal knowledge accepting new information from 'out there'. We are actively involved in the process and in fact invest new meaning in our experience of the world. As the authors of a recent report so aptly put it, "knowledge has been made... and can be remade".[40] Knowledge is therefore in an important sense **personal**. Second, knowledge evolves and changes through a constant process of debate and discussion between individuals. Knowledge is therefore in an important sense **interpersonal**. Both the personal and interpersonal aspects of knowledge demand the learning and application of skills. In order to elaborate on this a little further I shall refer to two writers in particular, Michael Polanyi and Karl Popper.

In Polanyi's view knowledge requires skill as well as pure thought. Knowing must incorporate the skill of knowing how. He writes, "I regard knowing as an active comprehension of the things known, an action that requires skill".[41] In addition, says Polanyi, skills cannot be fully accounted for, cannot be broken down to provide a step by step guide which students can learn by rote. There is always something more which is unspecified, a personal element which defies definition. They cannot be passed on in books or by instruction. "An art which cannot be specified cannot be transmitted by prescription, since no prescription for it exists."[42] To make the point Polanyi decribes the basics of learning to ride a bicycle. The principle, he says, by which the cyclist keeps his balance is not generally known. It is, "adjust the curvature of your bicycle's path in proportion to the ratio of your imbalance over the square of your speed."[43] Clearly we would never learn to ride a bicycle if all we did was to learn this. Simply following this rule would result in inevitable failure, together with a few bruises and skinned knees. Similarly, for example, with learning to investigate and evaluate. It is useful to know that investigating involves a number of stages such as planning, conducting and writing a report, or that evaluating is about weighing up possibilities and being able to justify your conclusion. But none of this is sufficient for developing such skills. Students can only learn by doing. For Polanyi the active participation of the learner is essential for learning. This active participation consists in the practice and development of skills.

While Polanyi stresses participation, Karl Popper brings out the importance of imagination and dialogue. According to Popper we do not obtain our knowledge of the world primarily through observation because there is no such thing as pure observation. Our observations are always interpreted in terms of our expectations and intentions. We always observe things because we already have an interest in them, have formulated questions about them, or formed beliefs and assumptions about them. Popper claims we are continually forming hypotheses and theories to solve problems which arise within our experience.

"The process of learning, of the growth of subjective knowledge, is always fundamentally the same. It is imaginative criticism... that is, test situations, critical situations; and by trying to locate, detect, and challenge our prejudices and habitual assumptions.... Seen in this light, life is problem-

solving and discovery - the discovery of new facts, of new possibilities, by way of trying out possibilities conceived in our imagination."[44]
For Popper, however, no theory can be finally true. We can only reach an approximation of the truth. Later evidence or new facts may cause us to alter our theories or even to reject them, but the process of discussion and dialogue leads to new ideas and points towards new theories.

"Popper's notion of 'the truth'is very like this: our concern in the pursuit of knowledge is to get closer and closer to the truth, and we may even know that we have made an advance, but we can never know if we have reached our goal."[45]

2. *Nature of learning and the learner.*

A recent headline in the Times Educational Supplement read, "HMI's want pupils ready for life of rapid change." The article was reporting a recent DES publication on careers and guidance. The report stated that children need to be prepared for a life of "rapid, challenging and at times uncomfortable economic and social change." This was probably never more necessary than today in a country still in the midst of the so-called Thatcherite revolution. Over the last decade few of Britain's most hallowed institutions have remained untouched by the hand of reform. We have experienced or are about to experience radical change within almost every area of our social life; health, education, local government, relationships at work, even our system of law. Not all change, however, is so visible. There has been, it would seem, some weakening of class barriers. A Mori study points to the fact that in May 1979 two-thirds of the British were rated by their jobs as working class and one-third middle class. Now four in ten households are rated middle class, a swing of seven per cent. Women too have improved their position. One third of the self-employed are female. In 1975, only 4 per cent of trainees for bank management were women, now 25 per cent succeed.[46]

So what kind of education system is best suited to such a rapidly changing society? Carl Rogers argues that any system of education which is geared to the imparting of knowledge is more suited to an unchanging environment rather than a fast changing one. Such an environment instead should concentrate on educating people to understand and cope with change, as well as developing the skills which will enable them to educate themselves. He writes, "The only man who is educated is the man who has learned how to learn; the man who has learned how to adapt and change; the man who has realised that no knowledge is secure, that only the process of seeking knowledge gives a basis for security."[47] Many, I'm sure, would want to complain that Rogers here has overstated his case. Is the question, 'What should we teach?' not an important one? Is it not a question which the professional has a duty to answer? And if not the professional alone, at least the professional in partnership with parents? Many have been incensed recently at the apparent substitution of the professional and parents by the government of the day in deciding national curriculum. But amid all the rhetoric what Rogers really wants is a change of emphasis in the direction of process. More reliance on process as opposed to knowledge of facts is what is required. For students to know the prevailing view on current political and social change, for them to understand Christian viewpoints on a variety of ethical and doctrinal issues is not sufficient. They must also learn how to acquire the information, and once acquired, to make responsible and informed judgements based on personal relevance, or using ethical, historical and other criteria.

Thinking and research regarding the nature of learning and the learner points to the important insight that children, whether we recognise the fact or not, are actively involved in their own learning. The view of the learner that emerges from the work of writers such as Jerome Bruner and David Ausubel is a 'constructivist' one. That is, that youngsters will think for themselves, will make sense of their experience, no matter what we do in schools. One of the priorities within education then should be to develop and sharpen those skills which make such activities possible.

Recently researchers spent time with mothers and children, taping conversations in their own homes. This showed, perhaps not surprisingly, that young children asked a tremendous number of questions. The researchers concluded that a significant proportion of questions asked by four to five year olds were what they called 'curiosity ' questions. These were questions prompted by children's puzzlement when faced with facts or events which did not quite fit what they already understood.
> "It seemed to us... that the children asked questions because there was a great deal that they did not know about the world, and many occasions when they were conscious of ignorance, misunderstanding and confusion. Often, the questions which we categorised as 'curiosity' questions occurred during conversations in which the child was deeply involved in struggling to understand her world"[48]

Violet Madge in her book 'Children in Search of Meaning' makes a similar point when she talks about children striving to integrate facts and ideas from all different areas of experience. There is no division into the sacred and the secular in the minds of young chidren.
> "Young children will attempt to integrate whatever comes into their experience into a meaningful pattern, be it angels and magnets, sun and rockets, seeds and babies, aeroplanes and heaven, God and shops, Jesus and baby-sitters."

I had an example of this from my own son. Once when he was about five years old and just started school, he said, "Daddy, do you think God helps the trees to grow?" Rather hesitantly I answered with, "Yes, I'm sure He does." There was a long pause, then my son exclaimed with a note of triumph, "But He doesn't plant the seeds, the Council does that!"

The studies and research of Nisbet and Shucksmith suggest that in becoming more aware of how we learn we can become more successful learners. This means that as part of setting up learning activities teachers should on occasions give students an opportunity to explore how best it can be tackled. For example when setting up a mini-investigation teachers could discuss with the class the various skills they will need. In particular she could discuss with them sources of information, reminding them about how to locate books in the library, about the importance of using an index, as well as the possibility of conducting interviews and surveys. A set of guidelines would be helpful here outlining the successive steps involved at each stage of an investigation, the planning, conducting and finally presenting the report. But in addition students need to assess continuously the relevance of information they collect, monitor their own progress so that they can identify weaknesses and ask for help if required, and revise their work in the light of new information. It is 'learning strategies' like these, say Nisbet and Shucksmith, that will mark the difference between good learning and poor learning.

> "We use the term 'strategies' to indicate a level above that of skills, putting the skills together."[49]
>
> "They seem to be more general in nature, the sorts of activities (like planning and checking) that are going to be needed time and time again in all sorts of different situations and problems."[50]

The following are some of the strategies mentioned by Nisbet and Shucksmith:

- Asking questions — defining hypotheses, formulating issues, establishing aims.
- Planning — deciding on tactics and timetables, reducing a task into its component parts.
- Checking — preliminary assessment of progress and results.
- Revising — may be simply re-drafting or it may involve a reconsideration of initial questions and goals.

Strategies then are essentially sequences of skills rather than isolated actions. Planning, conducting an investigation, and presenting a report are strategies in that they each involve putting together a series of skills in order to produce the desired result. Viewed in this way, doing a 'project' or 'investigating' an issue is no simple task and will require much practice if students are to learn effectively.

NOTES AND BIBLIOGRAPHY

1 *Moral and Religious Education in Scottish Schools*, SED, 1972.
2 ibid. 5.1
3 ibid. 4.32
4 ibid. 4.32
5 ibid. 8.4
6 Bulletin 1, *A Curricular Approach to R.E.* HMSO, 1978, para 3.1
7 ibid. para 7.1
8 ibid. para 7.2
9 Bulletin 2, *Curriculum Guidelines for R.E.* SCDS, 1981, para 2.3
10 ibid. para 4.2
11 *A Groundplan for the Study of Religion* Schools Council, 1977
12 Hampshire Agreed Syllabus, 1978
13 Hertfordshire Agreed Syllabus, 1981, and *Religious Heritage and Personal Quest*, 1982
14 Working Document, *Developing the R.E. Curriculum*, SCCORE, 1983
15 Religious Studies, Draft Grade Criteria, Secondary Examinations Council,1986
16 ibid. paras.2.3 and 2.4
17 *Suggestions for Curriculum Material in R.E.* SCCORE, 1984, p.6,7
18 *The Westhill Project R.E.5-16, How do I Teach R.E.?* Mary Glasgow,1986,p39
19 ibid. p42
20 ibid. p39-40
21 John Sealey, *Religious Education: Philosophical Perspectives*, Allen and Unwin, 1985, p49.
22 ibid. p49
23 See for example, Mary Simpson and Brian Arnold, *Diagnosis in Action*, Aberdeen College of Education, 1984.
24 See chapter 4
25 Gordon Kirk, *Curriculum and Assessment in the Scottish Secondary School*, Ward Lock, 1982, p5
26 ibid. p3
27 *Tell Them From Me*, Gow and McPherson,ed. Aberdeen University, 1980
28 Draft Grade Criteria, op.cit para 3.1
29 ibid. para 3.5
30 *Attainment in RE, A Handbook for Teachers*, 1989, The Regional RE Centre, Westhill College, Birmingham.
31 At the time of writing a report isbeing prepared in Scotland setting out Attainment Targets for students aged 5-14 years; (in Scotland the Attainment Targets are equivalent to the Attainment Statements in the Westhill Handbook). Operating within a national framework these targets are being devised across five levels of achievement, A - E.
32 *Assessment in Standard Grade Courses, Proposals for Simplification*, Scottish Education Department, 1986, para.4.12
33 Peter Kimber, 'The Scottish Experience', in Secondary Education Journal, NUT, November 1986
34 *The Observer* 20 August,1989
35 Assessment in Standard Grade, op.cit para.2.11
36 See Denis Lawton, *Class, Culture and the Curriculum*,1975
37 Philip Phenix, *Realms of Meaning*, McGraw Hill, 1964, p6f
38 Paul Hirst, 'Liberal education and the nature of Knowledge', in *Knowledge and the Curriculum*, RKP, 1974, p46
39 J.P.White, *Towards a Compulsory Curriculum*, RKP, 1973
40 *Education 10-14 in Scotland*, CCC, 1986, para.5.46
41 Michael Polanyi, *Personal Knowledge*, RKP, 1958, pvii
42 ibid. p.53
43 ibid.
44 Karl Popper, *Objective Knowledge*, OUP, 1972, p148
45 Brian Magee, *Popper*, Fontana Modern Masters series,
46 The Times, Tuesday April 11, 1989
47 Carl Rogers, *Freedom to Learn*, p 104
48 Tizard and Hughes, *Young Children Learning*, Fontana, 1984, p107f
49 J.Nisbet and Janet Shucksmith, *The Seventh Sense*, SCRE,1984, p9
50 J.Nisbet and Janet Shucksmith, *Learning Strategies*, RKP,1986, p26

2 AN APPROACH TO LEARNING

Looks at the importance of organising facts in order to achieve meaningful learning, before surveying a variety of conceptual schemes for structuring Religious Education. Different views of learning are examined and the main causes of student's failure to learn are described.

LEARNING FACTS

Some at least of today's concern about education stems from a feeling that traditional ways of teaching are being ignored in the rush to take up 'new' methods. A similar concern was evident in the sixties within primary education when the debate polarised around traditionalists and progressives. Today the argument traverses both primary and secondary and has surfaced in relatin to GCSE, Standard Grade and the National Curriculum. The situation was poignantly summarised recently in the Observer:

"Mr Gradgrind's approach to education is back in vogue. The Dickensian schoolmaster who demanded facts, facts, facts has won new supporters in a reaction against the trend towards learning skills."[1]

As we saw in the last chapter, there are good grounds to support the move away from learning facts towards developing skills within education. The facts themselves are not so important, it is argued, it's how we acquire them and what we do with them that counts. Hence the eighties have seen the emergence of examination courses north and south of the border stressing understanding, research skills and the ability to evaluate. Today's examinations are to some extent a reaction against earlier examples which on the whole concentrated on facts and factual recall. During the seventies and eighties in Scotland many subject teachers became dissatisfied with the 'O' grades which seemed to place too much emphasis on the assessment of knowledge. It would be an exaggeration to claim, however, that in the new courses facts are being ignored. In Religious Studies Standard Grade students are required to "identify or state significant facts" with respect to Christianity and one other world religion. In Standard Grade history, as well as learning skills, students are required to develop "knowledge and understanding of the variety of factors which have helped to shape the world in which they live." In GCSE Religious Studies the National Criteria state that the examination is out to test how far candidates are able to "select and present relevant factual information in an organised manner."

David Ausubel

Facts are essential. Without facts basic skills of reasoning and application would be impossible. But facts should not be taught in isolation, as if they were ends in themselves. They should be taught in relation to the underlying concepts and issues which give them their meaning. One prominent theory of the learning and retention of meaningful facts is that of David Ausubel. According to Ausubel, meaningful new ideas are learned by being linked to already existing concepts and propositions. Meaningful learning takes place as we try to make sense of new information or new concepts by making links with our existing knowledge and experience.

> "If we had to reduce all of educational psychology to just one single principle we would say this: Find out what the learner already knows and teach him or her accordingly."[2]

Ausubel educes a number of principles which he claims can facilitate meaningful learning. First, students should be made familiar with the central unfying concepts within the area of study before further related ideas are introduced. He believes that it is possible to identify key concepts or anchoring ideas in every topic. Second, when organising and presenting new material teachers must have regard to the limiting conditions imposed by general developmental readiness. For example, it is only at secondary level, says Ausubel, that a qualitatively new capacity emerges. The individual becomes capable of handling abstract relationships and of using hypotheses without reference to concrete examples.[3] Third, learners must be encouraged to reformulate new ideas and propositions in their own words. This helps to ensure that the relevant aspect of knowledge or experience is modified in the light of the new information. Fourth, teachers should make use of "advance organisers". These are initial summaries which provide frameworks linking together concepts and relationships which are to be explained later. The presentation of more detailed information is preceded by general principles and relationships to which it is related.

In the examples below, information about the celebration of Christmas, social concern, and material from Luke's gospel, is all seen to be related to Christian belief in the Incarnation. In turn these relationships are all subsumed under the common principle that a religion's key concepts are to be understood by reference to its scriptural sources and practices.

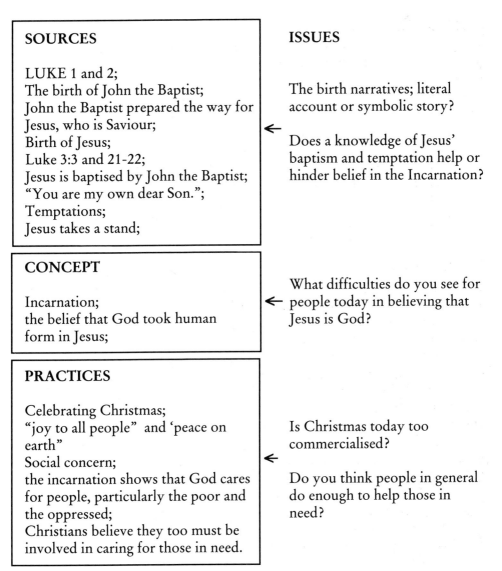

SOURCES

LUKE 1 and 2;
The birth of John the Baptist;
John the Baptist prepared the way for
Jesus, who is Saviour;
Birth of Jesus;
Luke 3:3 and 21-22;
Jesus is baptised by John the Baptist;
"You are my own dear Son.";
Temptations;
Jesus takes a stand;

ISSUES

The birth narratives; literal
account or symbolic story?

Does a knowledge of Jesus'
baptism and temptation help or
hinder belief in the Incarnation?

CONCEPT

Incarnation;
the belief that God took human
form in Jesus;

What difficulties do you see for
people today in believing that
Jesus is God?

PRACTICES

Celebrating Christmas;
"joy to all people" and 'peace on
earth"
Social concern;
the incarnation shows that God cares
for people, particularly the poor and
the oppressed;
Christians believe they too must be
involved in caring for those in need.

Is Christmas today too
commercialised?

Do you think people in general
do enough to help those in
need?

Ausubel argues that such a framework in advance helps students to see where more detailed information fits later. They can much more easily carry around such a framework uncluttered by a mass of detail. By drawing students' attemtion to the interrelationships, it can help them realise that it is meaningful learning which is important. Such meaningful learning is characterised by understanding rather than knowledge or isolated facts, and depends on a growing ability to see relationships rather than simply memorise. In addition, organisers help to highlight the differences between new learning and previous learning which may be similar and likely to cause confusion. In a recent examination we asked candidates about aspects of Luke 1 and 2 which Christians might use to support their belief in the Incarnation. Many answered using examples from other parts of the gospel.

Jerome Bruner

Like Ausubel, Jerome Bruner lays great stress on the importance of careful organisation of concepts and principles:

> "the curriculum of a subject should be determined by the most fundamental understanding that can be achieved of the underlying principles that give structure to that subject."[4]

Bruner believes that any body of knowledge can be presented in a form simple enough for any particular learner to understand. This can be done by matching the knowledge which the teacher wants the student to acquire with the student's stage of development. The structure of this knowledge may be characterised in three ways:

1   the mode of representation in which it is put;
2   its economy;
3   its power.

Each of these will vary in relation to different ages, to different preferred ways of learning among students, and to different subject matters.

• The mode of representation will relate particularly to the student's stage of development and will move dependence on concrete activities to abstract concepts and general principles. Infants and lower primary children will learn mostly by exploring their own experience of the world around them and developing their understanding of the feelings and thoughts which this produces. Children in upper primary and early secondary will gradually widen their horizons as they begin to see other people in a more objective and detached way. They will delight in observing the way people behave and in gathering information about their use of symbol and ritual to express important ideas. In upper secondary the emphasis will be on developing a range of more abstract concepts, although still based on concrete examples of sources and practices to which they relate.

• Economy refers to the amount of information a student has to work with in order to achieve understanding. For example, it is more economical to refer to the Incarnation as 'the belief that God took human form in Jesus' or to the relationship between Jesus and John the Baptist as 'John the Baptist prepares the way of Jesus who is Saviour'. Both of these, however, need considerable unpacking before students can understand their significance for Christians. Sudents need to begin therefore at a stage of less economy by exploring and selecting the significant facts within the sources.

• The power of any particular way of structuring knowledge resides in its capacity for enabling the learner to make connections and establish relationships between matters which otherwise might remain separate. It is at this point that a clear similarity emerges between Bruner's ideas about structure and the advance organisers suggested by Ausubel.

Paying attention to structure in this way is important, says Bruner, for a number of reasons. First, understanding fundamentals makes a subject more

comprehensible. For example, once students grasp that when
celebrate they are expressing what is important to them, then
simpler to see the point of some of the rituals connected with
festival of Diwali or the Christian festival of Easter. Second, ι
information are presented in a structured way they are quickly forgotten.
Hence the value of beginning with an overview of a topic or area of study
showing its essential features and interrelationships. This not only makes
clear to students what they are about to do, but also links it with what is to
come. Third, an understanding of fundamental principles and ideas can
facilitate learning from one topic or unit to another. For example, if a student
can understand that a religion's insights into the fundamental questions of
human life are expressed in its key concepts; and that these concepts can be
explored through the more concrete aspects of the religion such as its
scriptures and festivals, he or she will be better equipped to find his or her
way around any religion now or later in school or adult life.

For Bruner, however, understanding the basic structure is a subject is not just
a matter of coming to terms with the key concepts of that subject and the
network of relationships flowing from them and between them. He writes:
> 'Mastery of the fundamental ideas of a field involved not only the grasping
> of general principles but also with the development of an attitude toward
> learning and inquiry, towards guessing and hunches, towards the
> possibility of solving problems on one's own.'[5]

For Bruner, mastery of facts and relationships is inextricable linked to the
development of abilities, particularly those abilities which enable students to
go beyond the material evidence before them, to inquire into and to suggest
new ideas and possibilities. These are the roots of students' growing ability
of make judgments. But they must be nurtured. They must form an integral
part of planning for learning and teaching. We must somehow enable
students to develop their powers of thinking, "to generate good questions and
to come up with interesting informed guesses".[6] I will return to this issue
when dealing with evaluation. Meanwhile we need to look now at the idea of
'structure' as it has been applied within religious education.

STRUCTURE IN RELIGIOUS EDUCATION

"From the point of view of education what is essential is the grasp of a
conceptual scheme for ordering facts rather than skill in research".[7] Although
most teachers today would want to emphasise the development of research
skills in their students, R.S.Peter's point about the importance of structure is
nevertheless a crucial one. Indeed any survey of religious education over the
last two decades will quickly reveal that this is a point well taken by those
involved in that subject. Rationales and conceptual schemes abound.

the most famous of these is undoubtedly that of Ninian Smart who suggested that the study of religion should contain reference to a range of 'dimensions' namely, the doctrinal, mythological, ritual, social, ethical, and experiential. The Open University, on the other hand, in its approach to the study of religion, recommended a structure based on three interrelated questions, From what, To what, By what. These questions presuppose a clear soteriological pattern to the world's great religions and claim that the most appropriate method of studying these is to observe the human condition (from what), discover within a religion the goal of life (To what), and investigate how that goal is to be achieved (By what). More recently the National Criteria for G.C.S.E. have included a conceptual scheme based on key concepts and terms, special people and writings, principal beliefs and their relation to practice, responses to moral issues, and questions about the meaning of life. In his book' Problems and Possibilities for Religious Education', Edwin Cox outlines a structure particularly for the secondary school. It highlights such features as understanding ourselves (the personal aspect of religion), making ourselves useful (the communal aspect), how we treat others (the moral aspect), and meaning and significance (the doctrinal aspect).

In Scotland the Central Committee on religious education identified the distinctive features of religion as Transcendence, Communication, Relationship, Response and Meaning. And in one of the most developed attempts to perceive structure in religious education Alex Rodger and Elizabeth Templeton identified what they called basic or fundamental categories of religion, that is, "categories which structure, organise, give coherence"[8] to the mass of concrete phenomena found in religions. These were worship, salvation, interpretation, identity, and truth.

So how does a teacher choose between these different conceptual schemes? Clearly they are not simple alternatives. They imply different views of the nature of religion and religious education. Smart's approach for example emphasises understanding observable religious phenomena from the viewpoint or perspective of an adherent. Cox puts the emphasis on the individual's search for meaning and value, while the Open University and Roger/Templeton approaches are concerned with identifying the fundamental character of religion as the basis of a conceptual structure for religious education.

Whichever structure one chooses it will need to contain some reference to what is central to religion in order to provide direction for organising the curriculum. There is no necessity, however, to define religion or work out its most fundamental aspects before beginning the process of learning and teaching. In a recent book John Hick has stated that "religion takes such widely different forms and is interpreted in such widely different ways that it cannot be adequately defined but only described."[9] He proceeds to view religion as a "family-resemblance concept." By that he means that religions possess similar characteristics although there are no characteristics which every member must have in order to be part of the family of 'religion'. Nevertheless the existence of these similar characteristics distributed here and there and in varying degrees together distinguish this from a different family. The question of 'what is religion' can be part of the process of exploring the subject matter. Jean Holm, I believe, touched on something important in her now well known aim for religious education- "to explore what religion is and what it would mean to take a religion seriously".[10] Her statement points to the idea that any final answer to that question must remain open-ended at least for the duration of the study. It is a destination we may well arrive at rather than a place from where we start. And this is as true for teachers as it is for students. Certainly there is no absolute structure waiting to be uncovered. Since religions are dynamic changing systems their structure is also likely to be subject to change. Bruner himself makes the point that "the optimal structure of a body of knowledge is not absolute but relative."[11]

The Joint Working Party for the Scottish Standard Grade in Religious Studies similarly chose not to go down the road of stating fundamental categories of religion or trying to identify the essence of religion. I think there were two reasons for this:

1. We felt first of all that there was not yet a sufficient consensus on what were the fundamental categories of religion. Indeed, the process of comsulting teachers, which took place prior to the issuing of the final arrangements for Standard Grade, indicated that there was far from being a consensus on what were the key concepts of any one particular religion.

2. We were interested primarily in a different kind of structure. We were interested in finding a structure which would function at the level of the students and which could more immediately contribute to their learning. We were interested also in a structure which students could be informed about and which could be the source of realistic goals at which to aim.

Instead through its choice of content areas, the Joint Working Party first of all made a statement about what it regarded as appropriate for study by youngsters in the 14-16 age group. This included Christianity, one other world religion, issues of belief and issues of morality. It then proceeded to devise a structure for teaching religion based on the identification of key concepts within each religion. This structure is outlined in a series of important paragraphs in the Joint Working Party's report as follows:
   "The course is designed to help pupils to explore questions about religion...

questions about relationships, suffering, death, the existence of God."
"A religion's insights into these questions are expressed in its key concepts.
These concepts attempt to bring order and structure to the insights and
allow the development of a coherent and comprehensive view of the
meaning, value and purpose of life.

"Religious concepts are, however, expressed in a technical language not
readily understood by those outwith the religious communities. The
concepts may therefore be more readily explored by means of the more
concrete aspects of the religion which provide a rich and varied way into
the study of the subject..."[12]

The structure as set out above has a number of important features worth
noting:

1. It is based on identifying key concepts within each religion. For
Christianity they are Incarnation, Kingdom of God, and Resurrection. For
Judaism they are Torah, Covenant, and Deliverance. In Islam, God,
Revelation and Submission were selected and within Hinduism, Samsara,
Karma, Dharma, Moksha and God/Gods. These concepts are not intended to
be the only concepts which might form the basis of a course. They are
intended merely to represent a degree of shared understanding within each
relig ous community and to provide a window into that understanding for
others. Knowledge and understanding of concepts is to be developed by
exploring the more concrete aspects of the religion within sources and
practices. For example, a Christian understanding of resurrection will be
built up gradually through examining the resurrection story in Luke's gospel,
and how its significance is expressed in worship. Exploration of sources and
practices will normally reveal a variety of meanings indicating that the
concept is interpreted in different ways within that community of faith. To
begin with, however, a working definition of the concept will be sufficient.

2. It is primarily intended as an aid to students' learning. It first of all serves
to create a method for the study of religion which highlights the importance
of concepts and relationships rather than isolated facts. Secondly the
structure can also function as an 'advance organiser' showing students the
area they are working in at any time and how it relates to what has already
been done as well as what is to come. Students should therefore be made
familiar with such 'organisers' before starting work relating to a particular
concept. This structure, therefore, sits comfortably at the level of the
students and is in marked contrast to those we looked at earlier which tend to
be understood by teachers and perhaps only a minority of students. A few
quotes from the Rodger/Templeton scheme will make this clearer. Elizabeth
Templeton writes:

"Pupils... may not be aware at all of the second order categories."

"... studying this or that phenomenon (they) will be building up a grasp of categories which perhaps only the teacher can formally articulate". "It may be that only a limited proportion of pupils can manage this level of abstraction".[13]

Since this structure and the others mentioned above appear to be operating on a different level from the one being discussed within the context of Standard Grade they need not be seen in opposition to it.

3. It is concerned with 'ISSUES' as well as concepts. Issues may arise from examining sources or from a knowledge of practices or be related to questions about the relevance of a particular concept to the human search for meaning and value in life. Students will be expected to express and justify their own opinions on a range of such issues within each of the religions studied. This will inevitably involve them in the process of looking critically at their own beliefs and values. In this way we can engage them more personally in the study of religions in the expectation that they will learn from religion as well as about religion.

The structure is designed to help all students to learn more effectively and contains within it an assumed hierarchy of understanding. For example, it is assumed that students will find it more difficult to give an explanation of the key concept 'incarnation', taking into account varieties of interpretation, than they will to provide a simple definition of that concept. It is assumed also at the lowest level of achievement that students will be able to provide simple explanations of the significance of practices. Whereas at the highest level they will be expected to demonstrate a developed explanation. This at least would appear to accord with common sense. But is it quite so obvious why students for the lowest level of achievement should not be asked to give a simple explanation of the relationship between incarnation and the Christian festival of Christmas, or to explain the context for the Good Samaritan story. Whether there is such a hierarchy of understanding involved in understanding religious concepts and, if so, whether the hierarchy is as we have described, it is far too early to judge. The criteria for different levels of achievement were not written on the basis of what students actually demonstrated but rather on what teachers and others believed they could demonstrate, on the basis of their professional judgement. It is likely that over the next few years experience will force a number of changes in these formative ideas.

In the remainder of this section I have first set out some criteria for knowledge and understanding in ascending order to show the progression from one level to another (see Table 1), followed by examples of questions which have been used to assess them.[14] In addition, I have included a few examples to show the development across the levels making use of the same aspect of the same religion (see Table 2).

TABLE 1

CREDIT

The candidate can give a developed explanation of key concepts, sources and practices, with reference to their context, significance and interrelationship, and to varieties of interpretation.

GENERAL

The candidate can identify or state significant facts related to sources and practices, and can give an explanation of their context, significance and relationship to key concepts.

FOUNDATION

The candidate can identify or state significant facts related to sources and practices, and can give a simple explanation of their significance, as well as of associated terms and key concepts.

The Christmas card shows a scene from the story of Jesus birth.
What part is played in the story by
(1) angels, and
(2) shepherds?
Why do Christians think that the birth of Jesus is a happy event?

Why is water used in baptism?

"May your Kingdom come"
What do Christians mean by the Kingdom of God?

Christians call Jesus rising from the dead his Resurrection.
State two reasons why they believe the Resurrection is so important.

When Hindus worship at home they often use water. Explain how and why these are used.

What is Karma?

State two things Muslims normally do before they start praying.

Before they begin the pilgrimage, pilgrims have to put on white clothes called IHRAM.
Explain why they do this.

Why might Jesus' listeners have been shocked by the story of the Good Samaritan?

Outline the main details of the message which the angels gave to the shepherds.

What might Christians learn about the Kingdom of God from the stories of Jesus' miracles?

Explain the importance of the Covenant which the Lord made with the people of Israel.

Choose EITHER Brit Milah OR Bar Mitzvah and describe the rites associated with it.

What rules must a Muslim observe before he begins praying?

Why is the Qur'an so important for a Muslim?

Who was Rama and why is he thought to be the "ideal man"?

Describe one story connected with the festival of Holi.

What aspects of Luke 1 and 2 might Christians use to support their belief in the Incarnation?

What purposes are served by the Christian funeral service?

"Muhammed is only a messenger" (Sura 3.144)
Explain the importance of this statement.

Explain the Hindu concept of Moksha and how it relates to Samsara?

In what different ways is Torah understood in Jewish tradition?

TABLE 2

FOUNDATION	GENERAL	CREDIT
"May your Kingdom come" What do Christians mean by the Kingdom of God?	What can people learn about the Kingdom of God from stories of Jesus' miracles?	Explain fully the different ways in which Christians understand the Kingdom of God?
What do Hindu's mean by Samsara? Tick the correct box: Having many births ☐ Performing your duty ☐ Freedom from rebirth ☐	What do Hindus mean by Samsara?	Explain the Hindu concept of Moksha and how it relates to Samsara.
The following titles are used by Muslims to describe God. Which title means, 'God is Forgiving and Merciful'? Tick the correct box: Creator ☐ Compassionate ☐ All-Knowing ☐	In your own words explain what this passage teaches Muslims about God.	Choose two of the many names Muslims use for God. Explain what they teach Muslims about the character of God.
The Egyptian army eventually caught up with them "by the Red Sea". How did they escape from the Egyptian Army?	Describe briefly what Moses did to "seal the covenant".	What is the significance of Moses in the Exodus tradition?

LEARNING AND FAILING TO LEARN

The following letter appeared in the columns of a national newspaper.

EXAM FAILURES

Sir, In my schooldays (I am in my nineties) the children who failed in exams were thought to be those who did not try. This was not always true, but I still think that "trying" is the main attribute lacking in pupils who fail. Is this view hopelessly out of date?[15]

The writer has here put her finger on what is often considered an important cause of students failure to learn, namely, lack of effort. Comments on students degree of effort are often included in school report cards, carrying the implication that if only he or she could try a bit harder then success would be the inevitable result. e.g. "with a little more effort John has a good chance of passing his 'O' grade this year". But what does more effort mean? Does it mean 'spend more time studying', or 'pay more attention in class', or 'try to give more reasons for your answers instead of being satisfied with just one'?

The causes of such lack of effort are seldom investigated, probably because they are assumed to be mostly outside the teacher's control. Causes may range from lack of interest in a particular topic to lack of interest in school as a whole; from a personal family problem resulting temporarily in poor concentration to much more deep rooted personal and environmental factors such as emotional disturbance or social deprivation. They may be due to some disability as yet undetected or to persistent failure, where a student becomes so accustomed to achieving low grades that he or she sees little point in trying.

But to return for a moment to our alert ninety year old. She clearly feels that lack of effort was not always the main cause of pupil failure during her schooldays. Many would agree and would want to allude to a further cause best represented perhaps by a comment such as, "Mary tries hard but finds the subject difficult". What this seems to be saying is that despite trying hard Mary's level of attainment is still low in comparison with her fellow students. Mary is likely to conclude that she is 'not good at' mathematics or history or whatever. Indeed a few comments of this nature dotted around her report card and she could be forgiven for sitting back and giving up hope. The assumption here is that Mary possesses an innate level of general ability which is fixed and which determines her level of achievement. So no matter how hard she tries she is never going to achieve beyond that level.

Whether or not it makes sense to talk in terms of general intellectual ability is still the subject of much debate among psychologists. Eysenck, for example, has recently restated his view that general ability is largely inherited. He points to the consistencies in attainment which people show across differing intellectual tasks, as well as the correlation between IQ and patterns of brain activity as recorded on an electroencephalograph. Such results, however, are derived from population statistics and cannot be applied to individuals. As Eysenck himself says:

"...to state that 80% of the total variance of differences in intelligence in a given population are due to genetic causes cannot be taken to read that for a particular person 80% of his IQ is so determined;"[16] Most psychologists would want to stress that measured intelligence can change markedly over time if a child's family circumstances change in important ways. Recent research on the effects of divorce, for example, suggest that half of the children of divorced parents are under-achieving.[17]

Whatever the relative merits of this debate one fact remains. As teachers we have always observed in our classrooms a wide variation in students' attainments. Some students learn faster and more easily than others. Usually we have explained this phenomenon by saying that students evidently possess different amounts of general ability or different levels of intelligence. This

'fixed potential' concept of intelligence goes a long way to explain the attitudes of many teachers towards learning and learners. As a view of school learning it has two inherent dangers:
• First, it encourages us to take for granted the quality of our classroom preparation and organisation. If the main reason for students' failure to learn is lack of general ability then there is no need to examine closely the way we teach. We expect some students to perform well, some to perform moderately well, while the performance of others will be poor. And there's an end to it. Moreover if lack of general ability is the fundamental problem we do not need to concern ourselves too much with introducing a variety of teaching approaches in order to meet the different ways in which people learn. After all, moving from an approach in which the teacher does most of the talking to a more student-centered one where they are much involved in their own learning is not going to alter the basic facts of 'nature'.
• Second, it encourages us to set prior limits on students' achievements. Since we already know what John or Mary is capable of, based on either our own experience of them or on that of our colleagues, we can safely proceed to provide them with learning experiences which we believe are appropriate for them. Now, of course, it is eminently sensible to give students tasks which they are capable of achieving. These tasks match closely their previous learning and serve to enhance student confidence with all the likely attendant benefits for their future learning. What is not sensible and indeed is unacceptable, is that this is often all that we do. As a result we can justify all sorts of practices: for example, the separation of certain less able students from the rest of the class, either within the class, despite the presence of a learning support teacher, or as part of a policy of 'withdrawal'. On entering a class for the first time one learning support teacher was told, " Your students are the six sitting at the front".

An alternative view

Instead we might place the emphasis on each student's 'specific abilities', the collection of things that a student knows or can do at any particular time, rather than on the notion of 'general ability'.[18] A student's stock of these abilities can be thought of as building up gradually providing favourable conditions for successful learning. Those students who develop effective research skills, for example, or gain an initial understanding of basic concepts will be in a better position to take advantage of these and build on later learning. Those students however, who do not succeed in building up such skills and basic understandings, will tend to fall further and further behind.

It is particularly in the work of the American, Benjamin Bloom, that we see this view emerging. His research into 'mastery learning' makes "almost no assumptions about human capacity for learning. ...Much of individual differences in school learning may be regarded as man-made and accidental rather than as fixed in the individual at the time of conception."[19] Bloom's approach offers a much more optimistic view of what individuals can achieve and provides teachers with a way of thinking which avoids making assumptions in advance about what students can or cannot do. Nor do we need to tie ourselves up in a straitjacket in an attempt to conform to any popular images of 'mastery learning'. We need only give our support to a few key ideas. Bloom writes,

> "There are many versions of mastery learning in existence at present. All begin with the notion that most students can attain a high level of learning capability if instruction is approached sensitively and systematically, if students are helped when and where they have learning difficulties, if they are given sufficient time to achieve mastery, and if there are some clear criteria of what constitutes mastery."[20]

So what are the implications of taking on this fresh perspective? Most importantly, teachers must begin to view their students as individuals who possess a range of abilities rather than a fixed amount of intelligence. The introduction of courses and examinations for all students should help to promote such a view, although this will not happen without extensive in-service training. In a school I visited recently a head of department (not religious studies) was explaining to me how the assessment of investigative skills in his subject was, as far as he was concerned, a total failure, at least for the less able. The purpose of learning to investigate, he pointed out rightly, is to develop in students a degree of independent learning. And this, he said, is precisely what these students cannot do.

Specific abilities, however, will be more or less developed within any particular individual at any one time. If students are to develop their understanding of concepts, sources and practices, they will need to develop their abilities relating to enquiry and evaluation. Part of knowing and understanding is knowing how to acquire information and what to make of it. Students need successive opportunities to develop a range of these abilities within different contexts. They need to engage in research activities, for example, so that they can learn basic skills, such as where and how best to find information, as well as select out what is relevant. All students will require continual reinforcement in the development of knowledge and understanding. Gone should be the days when 'lesson plans' attempted to match up an objective to content and one or two activities. Effective learning for all students can only take place over a series of activities designed to reinforce one another through contact with a variety of resources. Students should be encouraged to express their opinions and justify them by means of open discussion and argument. The old addage 'practice makes perfect' is appropriate here, as long as the way is left open for all students to improve on their previous performance, to do better today than they did yesterday. This means providing them on occasions with tasks and activities which challenge them and force them to extend their previous performances. Over a two year course much may change in a student's life which influences his or her degree of motivation. Or a particular student may develop a special interest in part of the course, say issues of morality, with a consequent improvement in his or her grades.

Failing to learn

The discussion so far may draw the criticism that even with the best of intentions and the most effective classroom organisation students will not always learn what they are capable of learning, that what a student learns depends ultimately on the student. True, the factors influencing successful learning are far from being wholly under the teacher's control. But in the past we have surely exaggerated those factors which are outwith our control while paying scant attention to those that are not.

"It is only recently," says John Nisbet, "that we have begun to look for an explanation (for failure to learn) in terms of the actual teaching itself. Is the subject-matter properly ordered and appopriately matched to the learner's stage of development? Do the methods fit the mental equipment which the learner brings to the task?[21]

True, successful learning also depends on whether the student has an interest in the area being studied. This is not just a problem for the traditional presentation mode of teaching which, incidentally, can on occasions be extremely efficient. Resource-based learning and learning to investigate also depend for their effectiveness, and perhaps even more so, on well motivated learners. Such motivation may not be easily generated. Although this may be determined to some extent by extraneous factors, the teacher can make a contribution here by stimulating interest, through relating current activities to the wider study of the topic and encouraging students to look at the personal and social relevance of the material. Hence the value of structure and the raising of issues. Opportunities for students to assess their own progress and to discuss their difficulties openly with the teacher can also be significant.

Motivation, however, is a notoriously fragile entity easily disrupted by what might appear at first sight to be good practice. In a school I visited regularly the teacher on one occasion informed me that several students had decided not to sit the examination which all schools were due to run at the end of the first year of the course. They gave as their reason, inevitable failure. The teacher was more than a little disappointed. She had told them on many occasions that they need not worry about failing. Everyone received a grade related to how well they had done. What they had to do, therefore, was to turn in as good a performance as they could in order to obtain as high a grade as possible. 'Failure' was not really an option. In discussion with the teacher it emerged that she had been giving her students regular 'tests' in order to check their progress. In itself, an example of good practice. All students, however, sat the same test and she used raw scores, marking them out of a total of 20 or 30. As a result, the same students received low marks time and time again. Marks such as 4 out of 20, or 7 out of 30 were not uncommon. It is difficult to see what other conclusion the students could have arrived at apart from, "We have failed." In the light of this their eventual decision not to sit the examination seems entirely reasonable. In addition to the unfortunate use of marks here there was also a lack of differentiation in the use of the same test for all students. I will look more closely at the issue of differentiation in the following chapter.

I have argued that we must adopt a new perspective on learning if we are serious about promoting the education of all students, not just the brightest. Such a perspective will not solve every problem but it will, I believe, prevent us from making things difficult for many students. It is not sufficient to introduce 'resource-based learning', or 'individualised learning', or 'group discussion', although any one of these would be a step in the right direction. The new perspective requires a much more thorough-going review of the way we teach and organise learning in our classrooms. This is mainly because a significant part of students' failure to learn can be traced to this. Mary Simpson writes:

> "...research on pupil learning difficulties seems certain to confirm that many of these may be prevented by changes in teaching practice."[22]

Her research into the teaching of science has revealed two sources of learning difficulty which are associated with the way teachers teach rather than the way students learn. These are the inadequate development of concepts and the possession of wrong or inappropriate information. She found that students were being expected to understand complex scientific processes without having developed the simpler concepts which formed the basis of such understanding. As a result successful learning was denied to all but a minority of students. Learning takes place through the interaction of new information with existing ideas. If what students already know is inaccurate, then what is subsequently learned is also likely to be incorrect, unless specific measures are taken to put things right. Learning difficulties therefore can occur for the following reasons:

1. When presenting new information there may be nothing there for the new information to link up with. Alternatively, new information may connect with unsuitable ideas causing additional learning problems. In Religious Studies examinations students often confuse Passover with Communion and cite bread and wine as examples of food used in Passover, or talk about the

Passover wine as signifying the blood of Jesus. When asked about the religious significance of giving presents many will answer in terms of the gifts brought by the Magi rather than of the gift to the world Christians believe God made in Jesus as Saviour.

2. Sometimes students have an incorrect understanding of a concept or practice. In a recent 'O' grade examination there was widespread ignorance of 'sacrament' and a poor understanding of 'Holy Spirit'. In another, candidates seemed unaware that the reason why Muslims wash before beginning prayer has to do with ritual cleansing, and that it was not a prayer mat which was essential but a clean place.

3. At other times students will possess an alternative explanation of a concept which is perhaps more widely used. Such explanations are often difficult to shift. When asked about preparation for marriage in one examination candidates wrote about marriage in terms which related more to the wedding ceremony. They mentioned things such as 'where people should stand' and other details connected with the wedding rehearsal. Similarly the real nature of Christian love is frequently misunderstood, and discussed in terms of nice feelings instead of commitment.

NOTES AND BIBLIOGRAPHY

1 *The Observer*, March 5, 1989.
2 David Ausubel, Learning as Constructing Meaning, in *New Directions in Educational Psychology*, Falmer Press, 1985, p82
3 I have taken up this point in the chapter on evaluation.
4 Jerome Bruner, *The Process of Education*, Harvard University, 1966, p33
5 ibid p20
6 Bruner, *Toward a Theory of Instruction*, Harvard University, 1966, p33
7 R.S. Peters, What is an educational process? in *Standards, Schooling and Education*, Open University, 1980 p24
8 Alex Rodger ed. *A Conceptual Structure for Religious Education*, Dundee College of Education, p4
9 John Hick, *An Interpretation of Religion*, Macmillan, 1989, p5
10 Jean Holm, *Teaching Religion in School*, Oxford University Press, 1975
11 Bruner, Toward a Theory of Instruction, op.cit p41
12 Standard Grade Arrangements in Religious Studies, Scottish Examination Board, 1989, p4-5
13 Alex Rodger, op.cit p5
14 Questions are taken from Standard Grade Religious Studies Trial Examination, 1988, 89 and 90.
15 *Glasgow Herald*, September 1989
16 H.J.Eysenck, 'Heredity and Environment:The State of the Debate' in *New Directions in Educational Psychology*, op.cit p33
17 *The Observer*, Sunday 3 September 1989
18 Eric Drever, 'Mastery Learning in Context, Theory and Practice' in *Changing Face of Education 14-16*, ed. Sally Brown,Pamela Munn NFER, Nelson, 1985, p58

19 Benjamin Bloom, *Human Characteristics and School Learning*, New York, Harper, 1976, pp6,9
20 ibid. p4
21 John Nisbet, 'Changing Views on Ability', in *New Directions in Educational Psychology* op.cit p42

22 Mary Simpson, 'Diagnostic Assessment and it's Contribution to Pupils' Learning' in *Changing Face of Education*, op.cit p75

3 ORGANISING LEARNING

Describes research which indicates some difficulties relating to the organisation of learning. The importance of 'active' learning is emphasised through a discussion of independent and cooperative learning. The notion of differentiation is examined and some ideas offered about how it can be made effective in the classroom.

EFFECTIVE LEARNING

"There was no blackboard in the classroom, pupils sat on two long rows of sloping desks that faced one another while the master's taller desk was carefully placed close by the fireplace which was fed with peats brought by pupils... Each pupil struggled with problems and when he thought he had got the answer he would go up and show his slate to the master and if it was not right, go back to his seat and sit perhaps a day or two more on the same question".[1]

This was how a former student, James Skinner, described his experience of school in the small parish of Inverurie near Aberdeen, in the mid-nineteenth century. He noted, not surprisingly, that very little teaching had actually taken place. In 1873 members of the school Board visited the school for a day to watch some of the subjects being taught. Methods of teaching religious instruction left much to be desired.

"To the assembled classes able to read, the Bible is taught historically, the pupils being questioned as to their perception of the meaning of the statements read... In the younger classes the teacher reads the simpler Scripture narratives or gives short accounts of the biographies contained in them."[2]

Over a century later H.M. Inspectorate found that the most widely adopted approach in schools was whole class teaching. Regardless of subject they observed a great deal of uniformity of method from one teacher to another and from one school to another. The features most in evidence were "teacher talk, question and answer, and assignment in that order."[3] In justifying their class teaching approaches teachers argued that syllabuses were crowded and therefore it was necessary to concentrate on covering the content rather than trying to engage students in a wide range of time-consuming activities. Textbooks were still the most popular resource and teacher-talk the principal means of presenting their contents. Worksheets were in general use, their main function being to impart information..

Some recent research

Similar findings emerged from the investigation of mixed ability teaching conducted within the Teacher Education Project based at Nottingham University.[4] The Project team soon discovered a glaring discrepancy between the underlying philosophy of mixed-ability teaching and its practice. In theory mixed-ability organisation was intended to provide ways of catering for the needs of individual students through a greater use of group work and individualised learning. In practice definitions of 'mixed-ability' varied considerably. In some schools it excluded the least able while in others the mix was achieved only after the most able students had been selected out. Throughout, whole class teaching predominated and genuine group work was rare. Usually, group work consisted of students sitting together in groups of varying size but working individually on the same assignment. Tasks were relatively low level requiring little serious thinking, and resources were seldom suitable for the wide range of ability participating:

> "Many mixed-ability classes are in the whole class mode, with mainly undemanding and undifferentiated work aimed at, or a little below, the middle of the ability range."[5]

Where mixed-ability situations were being handled successfully, a key factor was flexibility on the part of the teacher. Teachers felt able to use a number of teaching styles, make use of a range of audio-visual media, and encourage a variety of student activities to proceed simultaneously. Among the factors contributing to such flexibility were size and layout of room, length of lesson and size of class, as well as available resources. The teacher's own skill and preferred style, and his or her perceptions concerning the students as a class were also important: Were they able to work quietly? Were they well motivated? Could they be trusted to work on their own?

The findings of the Project seemed to throw some doubt on the ability of this form of organisation to cater for all students, particularly the most able and the least able. All teachers reported problems with these two groups such as work being quickly finished, consequent boredom and lack of motivation, leading to disruption especially among the least able. Teachers were aware of the need to provide appropriate attention to both groups but were unable to do so.

In the primary school too, the use of small groups does not invariably result in the matching of educational provision to the needs of individuals. In a research project conducted among Scottish schools, 20% of the teachers observed taught arithmetic to two groups separately; 30% taught their classes in three or more groups, though here less than half had groups of 7 or less. The remaining 50% taught the class as a single unit. In language work 21%

taught two groups, while 18% taught three or more groups. The research further revealed that many of the teachers who used group methods showed little awareness of its purpose in terms of differentiated treatment for students. Arranging students in groups appeared to be more of an organisational device than an educational one. Most teachers had students sitting in groups, "but the observers very quickly learned that seating arrangements are a very poor guide to whether group methods are indeed being employed at all."[6] It was not uncommon, say the researchers, to find students seated in circular groups being taught from the front as a single group. In such a situation written work could just as effectively be carried out within the context of traditional rows.

"It was clear from the research that the number of teachers was small who used group methods in ways that secured from those methods advantages that it is difficult to or impossible to obtain otherwise."[7]

Some personal observations

In my own work with teachers, concern about how best to cater for individual students across a wide range of abilities was high on the agenda. At first many expressed the feeling that they did not have time to prepare sufficient material for extension or additional work. Some even expressed satisfaction that things were going alright, and in any case the range of abilities among their students was not very wide. This they felt obviated the need for differentiated treatment. Most teachers settled down to a situation in which all students were doing the same work with occasional additional work for those who had completed the initial activities. The additional work, however, often lacked purpose and was usually designed to fill the 'gap' created by the fast learners. It soon became clear that this was not sufficient, not only because students learned at different rates but also because there was no guarantee that students would be working at their best within common activities. Differentiated materials were required to stretch all students, the less able as well as the more able. This has proved to be a difficult and arduous task for teachers. Consequently regional development groups have been strongly eencouraged to include such differentiated materials within the support material they are producing.

Almost every school operated some form of group arrangement. Groups were usually based on friendship ties, rarely on the basis of ability. Some teachers changed groups around, depending on the nature of the task being done. Usually students seated in groups worked as individuals, although it was common to find teachers encouraging students to discuss their responses together before completing their individual tasks. Where this resulted in genuine discussion among students it proved to be a valuable experience. Also successful was where the teacher sat in with a group and took part in the e or she would encourage individuals to express their opinions, all the time to give reasons for what they said, and bringing in ers of the group by asking them to comment. It was rare, he o see a group working as a group to prepare a group product. There were few examples of group discussions in which a group produced a joint response to an issue, nor were the results of group discussion generally recorded in students' workbooks. Yet many teachers reported that they did a lot of discussion. And students themselves often confirmed this. A good deal of discussion took place with the whole class when it might have seemed advantageous to divide the class into smaller units.

Most schools involved their students in a variety of research work. Indeed this was probably the central means by which teachers saw themselves as entering into the spirit of the new course. Many teachers were concerned about whether they had the time to teach the necessary skills of inquiry, and whether there was likely to be a lot of duplication for students since many subjects were showing an interest in this area. A number of teachers though, soon reported important improvements particularly among the less able students, in their ability to locate information in books, use indexes, and generally take responsibility for their own learning. As one teacher remarked, "they have stopped coming out every ten minutes to say, 'I've finished Miss, what will I do now?'"

For effective learning a variety of learning and teaching approaches will be essential. When the task is to impart knowledge and understanding it is quite in order, although not always appropriate, for the teacher to adopt a presentation style of teaching in which he or she either talks to the whole class or makes use of audio-visual techniques to get across a certain body of information. When the task is to help students develop the skills of investigating an issue, of finding information, selecting and sorting out what is or what is not relevant, and drawing conclusions from the information available, a presentation style of teaching is no longer useful. In these sorts of tasks students need to be active rather than passive, doing things rather than having things done to them or for them. We cannot teach skills; students must learn skills by practising them.

According to the philosopher, Michael Oakshott, a distinction between 'information' and 'judgement' is essential to the business of learning and teaching, He maintains that, "there is in all knowledge an ingredient of information..." but "this ingredient of information... never constitutes the whole of what we know."[8] In addition to information we require that kind of knowledge which enables us to interpret information, to decide whether or not it is relevant, to go beyond the information and try out new possibilities and hypotheses. This form of knowing Oakshott calls judgement. It represents a range of skills and abilities which characterise the 'knowing how' component of knowledge. We may know how to do something without being able to state explicitly what is involved in the 'doing' of it. This has important implications for learning and teaching, says Oakshott, since unlike information, judgement cannot be passed on merely by instruction. "Learning," writes Oakshott, "is a twofold activity of acquiring 'information' and coming to possess 'judgement'... and these two components cannot be communicated in the same manner."[9]

As we have already noted, the work of both Polanyi and Popper point to the importance of active learning, of enabling students to become as actively involved in their own learning as possible. Someone once said to me that they thought the notion of active learning was an unnecessary one since even students who are sitting listening are actively involved. Well, who knows? Perhaps like Mr. Daydream they are visiting exotic places or reliving a recent adventure. In any case what I think people mean is that students should be less the passive receptacles of knowledge and more the active participants in acquiring that knowledge. The best description of active learning I know is contained in the HMI Report, 'Learning and Teaching in Religious Education'. It states:
"...a wide variety of methodology was in use and pupils learned through listening and speaking, researching and discussing. Sometimes they worked as a class, sometimes in pairs or in groups. They became familiar with learning from audio-visual material as well as from books, with recording what they had learned in their own individual style and, in discussion, with proposing solutions of their own and considering the views of their peers".[10]

A VARIETY OF APPROACHES

As teachers we have tended to develop certain styles of teaching which, as we have seen, are most appropriately directed at the whole class. We have become adept at the preparation of worksheets and, with the help of examination boards, at setting and marking examinations. We have often judged ourselves, and been judged by others, against the dubious standard of examination passes. The latter is sometimes used as an argument against change. As one teacher commented, "I've been teaching now for fifteen years and in that time I've had excellent pass rates. Why should I change the way I teach now?" We have sometimes viewed teaching skills in terms of our ability to manage a whole class without losing control. Being able to manage a class discussion successfully in which students only spoke in turn, refraining from eagerly shouting out their answers, was something to which I as a young teacher longingly aspired. Never mind that only a small percentage of students ever contributed or that learning was being continually subordinated to teaching.

"The simplest, and most insistent, message from the research literature," says Noel Entwistle, "is that there can be no single 'right' way to study or 'best' way to teach. The differences between people's abilities, cognitive preferences, and personalities are too great."[11]

This suggests that any attempt to rely on one style of teaching is doomed to failure because among other things people have different preferred ways of learning and will therefore benefit from exposure to variety in different ways. There would seem, to be at least four distinct ways in which people learn:

1. by receiving information and explanation from others, verbally, visually or in writing.
2. by cooperating with others to clarify ideas or argue out an issue.
3. by working on one's own to find information or solve a problem.
4. by direct experience of the things to be learned.

The first and third of these could be associated with a form of teaching which involves the whole class doing the same thing, at the same time and at the same pace. Neither of them of course need imply anything of the kind. The information being received may be different and graded according to level of difficulty. Only one group out of the whole class may be scrutinising a number of slides relating to, for example, Hindu puja. And the individual working on his own may be investigating his own chosen subject and operating at his own speed. Certainly, any attempt to employ the whole range of techniques would result in a considerable re-think of classroom organisation and layout. This is precisely what seems to have happened in the schools with which I was involved. The Joint Working Party report on Standard Grade Religious Studies stated that in order to teach the course effectively certain learning experiences were essential. These were 'Independent' learning experiences concerned with providing opportunities for students to develop responsibility for their own learning; and 'Cooperative', which was concerned with providing opportunities for students to work together. In addition the Working Party assumed that learning was essentially 'active' and included a list of activities covering both independent and cooperative learning, along with related examples to show the range of things that might be done. Among these were:

Role playing	A family discussion about a daughters unwanted pregnancy.
Group discussion	On whether there could be life after death.
Class debate	Is the taking of life ever justified?
Brainstorming	On beliefs about God.
Completing a worksheet	On the Five Pillars of Islam.
Watching an audio-visual presentation.	Watching a video of a baptism.

Researching opinions	Conducting a survey of students on euthanasia
Visit	To a Jewish synagogue.
Observer participation in community activities	Joining in a local celebration of a religious in festival such as Diwali.

Independent Learning

To develop the skill of independent learning students need practice at planning tasks, locating and selecting relevant information using a wide range of resources, as well as drawing their own conclusions and presenting them clearly. Independent learning is not about working in isolation. On the contrary, it involves being aware of difficulties encountered and knowing when help from the teacher is essential for further progress. It is about learning to cope with tasks and assignments without being continually guided and directed by the teacher.

"It is the developing ability to see and to use books, computer programmes, the teacher and indeed other adults, as resources for attaining the learning purposes".[12]

The encouragement of more independence in learning is an important part of the whole process of education, particularly education for personal autonomy, to which religious studies can make a significant contribution.[13] Within religious studies students need to develop the ability to pursue religious and moral questions with confidence not only in school but in life beyond school. For this they will need help in identifying different types of issues, in clarifying questions and in learning to evaluate.

Some time ago I had the pleasure of attending my first parent's evening as a parent. The teacher described how my son was building up his own vocabulary by writing stories using a word book. She had compiled it herself, and her students were using it like a dictionary to find, spell and write the words they wanted. She was in effect encouraging her students to develop certain access skills through which they could begin to build up their own knowledge of words. Just a tiny example but it seems to me to reflect something of the best of whats happening in many of our primary schools. I expect its the kind of thing which has led HM Inspectorate to write:

"Pupils in the primary schools are becoming more active in their own learning, self-motivated and independent, and accustomed to exercising a degree of choice in their activities."[14]

If students are to develop independence in learning as early as possible, they need to develop a range of skills which can serve to increase their capacity for learning. Among these are skills relating to the retrieval of information from a variety of sources. Particularly important are library and reference skills.

Students need to be able to make effective use of dictionaries, indices and contents pages, if they are to easily find the information they want. Of course students require plenty opportunities to practise and apply these skills in a variety of contexts. This means that they need to be engaged in research as part of their usual means of learning - finding information for themselves, going to the library, interviewing. This will not always be on large scale projects. They may be asked, for example, to find out from reading books or looking at slides how Muslims celebrate Id-ul-Fitr, or why Christmas is important to Christians. If a computer database is available they may be involved in a search for information relating to, say, different views about abortion.[15]

On the other hand we may be expecting something much more extensive and developed in terms of accessing and handling information. Presenting students with an issue on which there are different views or asking them to formulate an issue for themselves is the best way of proceeding here. This provides a purpose to the task of collecting information and a basis for relevant selection. It also means that students have to bring together many of the skills they have previously practised in isolation in order to achieve the required results. Here the skills of evaluating are as important as the skills of retrieving information. Much of the project work and enquiry-based learning in schools stops short at searching for and finding information. Thinking about ideas, making judgements and justifying opinions are very much part of the full process of enquiry. There are three main parts to the process of investigating issues - planning, conducting or carrying out the investigation, and presenting the results. These should be thought of as three discrete stages of investigating and treated as such for teaching and assessing. What is involved in each stage needs to be explained carefully to students before they begin. When it comes to assessment we need to remember that the processes of planning and conducting are as important as the final product. The following skills seem to be the most important:

Planning	choosing a topic, formulating an issue, asking questions, identifying resources, constructing a plan of action.
Conducting	locating and recording information, identifying and explaining different viewpoints.
Presenting	writing a report, expressing and justifying opinions and drawing conclusions.

It is helpful to think of learning as involving two stages. First, knowledge and understanding of what is to be learned, the course content. Second, revising that understanding in order to reinforce it and make it stick. Students can be taught skills and strategies for dealing with both these stages.[16] For example, in religious education, understanding involves learning about key concepts and how these are expressed within sources and current practices. Students can be shown how these are related, how to link this with what they already know, and to make notes about it in their own words. Revision involves recalling everything that is relevant and checking the result against original notes. Revision or reinforcement needs to take place soon after the initial learning. It is not something that can be left to the end of a unit or topic. Initial understanding might be brought about with the aid of techniques such as underlining and labelling. The purpose of such techniques is to help students select important information and identify it. The teacher might choose one or more texts for the students to work on. These might be scriptural passages or descriptions of a religious festival. The teacher might be interested in highlighting 'incarnation' within the birth narratives, or helping students to see the significance of bar mitzvah for Jews. Students will then underline those parts of the passages which are relevant to those issues or ideas. Having done this they should compare their work with a partner or in small groups in order to arrive at a consensus. Labelling or naming parts of a text can be carried out in a similar manner enabling students to distinguish, for example, between what happens during regular worship in the Roman Catholic Church, and its significance for the worshippers. Through these techniques students are not only helped to make sense of what they read but are left with a summary of their learning which they can use as a basis for other writing and revision.

The 'definitions game' is a useful activity for helping students to revise their learning and clarify their thinking before moving on to other related tasks and assignments. It can also provide the teacher with a useful means of checking whether students are still experiencing difficulties. The teacher identifies a number of concepts or viewpoints within a particular unit of work. Each concept or viewpoint is written on a separate card and distributed between different groups. Each person is given ten minutes to explain its concepts before being called upon to report to the rest of the class, who then have to guess the word or words on the card. In addition to guessing the concept or viewpoint, the rest of the class have to say how complete or accurate they regard the explanation, or whether there are aspects in need of further clarification. If appropriate they might also be asked to comment on the adequacy of a belief, for example, in terms of its relevance as a guide to everyday living, or to express and justify an opinion on the given viewpoint.

Co-operative Learning

This involves experiences in which students work together and learn from each other. They may be sharing tasks connected with gathering information and viewpoints or in debating issues. Through group work students can be given ample opportunities to talk things through with each other, to test out their ideas and to express and justify their own opinions.

Much energy is often expended on deciding the ideal basis for the formation of groups. Should students be encouraged to form their own groups based on friendship ties? Should teachers decide the groups? Should they be made up of students with similar abilities or should they contain an appropriate mix of abilities? Depending on the nature of the task, all of these options may be considered appropriate at one time or another. There is some evidence to suggest, however, that:

> "...groupings appear to be one of the least important factors for good discussion. I think the most important factors are that the children understand the task, that they see its relevance, that they understand how they will have to report back, and that if possible - they have something real to help focus their attention."[17]

The principal means by which co-operative learning takes place is talk. Until recently, most formal schooling seemed designed to prevent students from co-operating through talk. Students would be accused of cheating if caught talking to a neighbour. Even today among some teachers, individualised worksheets dominate the learning process making genuine collaboration and purposeful talk between students difficult or impossible to achieve. Often the only opportunity available to students to express their opinion is via a written question at the end of a worksheet. This practice of several tasks relating to the provision of information followed by an evaluation question is often reinforced by the use of a similar format in national examinations. Although this may be appropriate for the purposes of examining it is not sufficient for learning. Much more needs to be done by means of talk and discussion if students are to develop the confidence and ability to argue and debate.

Talk can also be important for the understanding of concepts and relationships. The process of assimilating new knowledge into existing knowledge and experience, of reshaping it to take account of new ideas and information is a necessary element in learning. Wherever there is a range of interpretations to be found, depths of meaning to be uncovered, different levels of explanation to be pursued, the opportunity to talk these through will be important. Such discussions will inevitably be hesitant and speculative, characterised by unverified supposition and frequent attempts to reorganise and rephrase. Hypothetical expressions such as 'its probably...', 'it could be...', 'perhaps she thought that...' will be the rule rather than the exception. Douglas Barnes writes:

> "I would argue that this kind of approach to learning should be encouraged, and that this cannot readily be done either in conventional teacher-class exchanges or by giving individual tasks to pupils."[18]

Group discussions, however, are by no means easy to organise. Success will not automatically follow from putting students into groups and leaving them to learn. It may be that successful group discussion becomes possible only after successful class discussions have served to reassure students that their comments and opinions are valuable. This demands in turn a particular attitude and approach to knowledge and learning. For example, Powell describes the teaching style of one primary teacher thus:

> "What was so striking about her pupils was that they were manifestly thinking as they framed their answers. They were encouraged so to do by her refraining from saying that an answer was wrong; instead, if she thought it was not altogether right, she would respond non-commitally in a tone that suggested to the pupil that he should go on thinking about what he had just said. In this way pupils were led to find faults in their own responses and amend them. Thus, for children in her class, knowledge and ideas were open-ended, originality was something to be valued, and their own views and interests counted."[19]

An important element in co-operative learning is the opportunity for the group to present its ideas and conclusions to the whole class. This can have a significant effect on the group. Members are now conscious of having to be much clearer in the way they organise their thoughts and conclusions since these have to be presented to others who have not been party to the discussion. This 'reporting back' will serve to iron out the tentativeness of much early dicussion forcing them to clarify some things while elaborating on others. Preparation too is vital not only in the form of a stimulus for the discussion but also to provide a 'point of return' if discussion falters or proceeds up a blind alley towards a dead-end. The following stages seem important for effective discussion.

1. **Preparation** The teacher introduces the stimulus for the discussion to the whole class. This might be a television programme, slides or an appropriate extract. He or she focuses the students' attention on the questions or issues they will need to consider. Preparation might also include reminding students of previous work done on the topic.
2. **Discussion** Students proceed to talk about the issues to which their attention has been directed, having appointed a secretary to take notes. The teacher may decide to set a time limit on the discussion.
3. **Consolidation** Students are given time to organise their ideas and conclusions for presentation to the whole class. Notes taken during the discussion will be examined by the rest of the group for their accuracy and altered or elaborated if appropriate.
4. **Presentation** One member is chosen to present the group's findings to the other students who are invited to ask questions and comment. This leads to further discussion involving the whole class.

on The group's findings are given a more permanent form by
ncluded as part of a wall-display, or being duplicated and handed
each member of the class.

This sequence of stages may seem a trifle idealised, concealing a number of
difficulties for both teachers and students. It certainly masks a great deal of
basic skills on the part of students which are essential for its smooth
operation. Skills such as the ability to listen carefully, to contribute ideas
without shouting, to build on other people's suggestions, to wait one's turn
to talk, to accept other people's ideas if they seem reasonable, to keep to the
point. Clearly, we cannot exclude group discussion until such skills have
been sufficiently developed. In any case they are best developed by methods
of active participation. A whole school policy in this area is as important as
in the area of enquiry and investigative skills.

For those of us who are hesitant about plunging in at the deep end, other
more supportive forms of talk might be attempted initially. Students might
be discussing in groups, but with the teacher taking a more active and
directing role at first. This allows the teacher to demonstrate the importance
of several key aspects of group discussion, for example; encouraging everyone
to contribute, ensuring that people stick to the topic, and avoiding the
discussion becoming bogged down too long on one point. The teacher can
introduce students to some useful ways of handling these situations. If one
person is dominating the discussion, someone might say, 'What does
everyone else think about this?' Quiet members of a group can be encouraged
by someone asking, 'How do you feel about that, John?' And the group can
be steered on to the next point by a statement like, 'Perhaps we should move
on now to...'

The technique of brainstorming is also a useful one for involving the whole
class. The students work in groups where the idea is for each member of the
group to think up as many ideas or pieces of information as possible about a
topic. Students are asked to keep the ideas coming but to refrain from
making any comment on them. Individual contributions are gathered
together without any attempt initially at categorising them or establishing a
priority. The main point is that students are encouraged to try out their ideas
without fear of being wrong or laughed at. The teacher should avoid the
temptation of jumping in whenever the flow of ideas seems to be drying up,
although there is no reason why he or she should not also contribute ideas.
When the brainstorm is complete, groups should turn to the task of thinking
a bit more critically about the ideas that have emerged, so that some basis for
choosing what is relevant or important is established. Brainstorming is a
useful and fun way of introducing a new topic or revising a previous one. It
can be used as a starter to a discussion, as a prelude to a written assignment,

or as a means of evaluating an activity just completed.

Finally, Brandes and Ginnis suggest a series of strategies for developing group work skills. Particularly important for raising confidence and developing listening skills is the 'round'. This is a time when each member of a group has

the opportunity to make a statement on the subject under discussion. Each person takes it in turn to speak, no one is allowed to comment on what is said, and no one is forced to speak when it is their turn. "The aim of the round is to provide a structure within which everyone has a chance to say something, but is not forced to do so. All ideas and opinions are valued equally."[20]

DIFFERENTIATION

In a recent book called 'Choosing a State School' the authors refer to mixed ability teaching as a situation "in which the slowest and brightest are taught together in one class - some say to the detriment of both in some subjects."[21] If the teacher works mainly from the front of the class, with teacher talk as the primary source of information, and all students expected to do the same work at the same time, then the phenomenon of 'teaching to the middle' will inevitably occur. As a result, able students will not be stretched while less able students will most certainly be left behind. For mixed ability teaching to be successful it must be good teaching. This is true also for teaching within so-called 'streamed' classes. I recall vividly my own schooldays sitting in a streamed class for mathematics. The teaching style consisted entirely of examples, with explanation, completed on the blackboard by the teacher. We students were then required to complete similar examples from the set textbook. After some time, usually determined by how long it took the most able students to complete the examples, the teacher moved on. On reflection this was not so much 'teaching to the middle' as 'teaching to the top'. I have no clear recollection of ever finishing an exercise given me by that teacher. I concluded from that experience that my future in mathematics was a decidedly gloomy one and turned my attention to other things.

But to return to the important question which seems to me to be raised by the authors of the book. Can learning be organised within a mixed ability situation so that all students have the opportunity to benefit? The code word for such organisation is '**Differentiation**'. Differentiation takes place whenever students are given the opportunity to learn at their own pace, or complete tasks appropriate to their current levels of performance. What I am concerned with here is differentiation within the learning and teaching process. I am not concerned with differentiation as it is reflected in the pattern of examination papers at the end of a course. For example, in G.C.S.E. Religious Studies that pattern is one of a common paper with stepped questions in ascending order of difficulty. Whereas in Standard Grade Religious Studies it is separate papers for each level. There is, of course, a close relationship between these in that student tasks and activities will need to mirror different levels of difficulty, but clearly any particular pattern of examination paper will not preclude the use of a variety of ways of differentiating.

Differentiation is not just essential within mixed ability groups but within any group where the intention is to develop the understanding and skills of all the participants. In the early stages of piloting Standard Grade, teachers were quickly aware of the need to differentiate across the three levels of achievement. A frequent question was, 'Do I need three levels of material to match these three levels of attainment? While some teachers did think of differentiation initially in terms of different levels of worksheets, others were more concerned to introduce differentiation through various types of group work and individual research. Indeed one of the first visible signs of change arising from implementation of the new syllabus was this movement from whole class teaching to group work. Teachers had quickly recognised the potential for variety that exists when students are permanently arranged in groups. Whole class teaching of course would still take place, for example, when it seemed appropriate to show a particular set of slides or television programme to everyone at the same time. But now teachers could much more easily vary the pace of learning using different resources for different groups or for different individuals within the same group. They could ensure that learning was being constantly reinforced through opportunities to discuss new ideas and express opinions. Finally they could create an atmosphere in which students' learning requirements were the driving force behind the teaching process. Students could learn at their own pace, while at the same time be encouraged to extend their existing abilities and develop new ones, by introducing a range of material tailored to meet the specific needs of individuals.

Core and extension

One of the most familiar ways of introducing such material is through '**core and extension**'. By 'core', teachers generally mean the minimum they can expect students to know or be able to do after having taught a unit or section of work. 'Extension' is usually taken to refer to work designed to 'stretch' the experience of those students who encounter little or no difficulty with the core. The 'core and extension' method usually carries the implication of providing remedial or reinforcement work for those students who were unsuccessful with the core work first time round. Using this method, a teacher will identify key ideas and skills with which he or she thinks all students should be familiar. Having taught the section, the teacher will then administer a test to determine which students have succeeded in the core and which have not. Those who have successfully completed the core will progress to extension exercises; for the others, appropriate remedial or reinforcement activities will be provided. The following diagram is an example of how this process might operate:

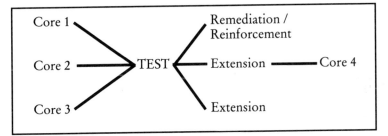

As a means of differentiating, however, 'core and extension' has a number of problems. First, how do we decide what is to be the core? Is it to be 'what we know all students are capable of' on the basis of our previous experience? Is it to be 'what we think all students *should* be able to do', thereby setting a minimum standard? Or should it be the minimum understanding necessary for entry into a particular course, for example, 'O' grade or at one time, G.C.E.? Second, the method seems to leave little room for development, particularly with regard to skills, which may be developing over the course as a whole. Suppose we decide that the minimum necessary in relation to 'evaluating', is that students 'can express an opinion supported by one valid reason'. In Standard Grade religious studies students who demonstrate this consistently over the course can expect a grade 5 or 6. But as students progress through the course, an increasing number of them may be performing at a higher level. In this case there seems little point in all students completing core work simply to demonstrate what they may already have shown on a number of occasions. Third, if the core has been set at too high a level some students may seldom, if ever, have the opportunity of moving on to extension work. If, in addition, the core is seen as merely a prelude to more advanced work, then over a period this will seriously damage motivation.

Open activities

In the light of such problems it would be more helpful if the 'core' were seen to constitute a worthwhile challenge for all students. To meet this requirement it would need to be understood not in terms of minimum content or learning objectives but in terms of student activities, the 'core activities' essential for fulfilling the aims and content of the course. All students would participate in these core activities demonstrating different levels of attainment within them. These core activities will be more accurately described as 'open activities' since they are designed to be tackled by all students. Differentiation will occur by outcome as students take the opportunity to find their own level of achievement. The following are examples of what we might call 'open activities':

- conducting a survey of fellow students on abortion;
- visiting places of worship and making appropriate notes;
- joining in the local celebration of a religious festival;
- group discussion on whether there is life beyond death;
- role playing a family discussion about an unwanted pregnancy;
- taking part in a class debate on whether war can ever be justified;
- watching and commenting on a video of an adult being baptised;
- preparing and conducting a Passover meal;
- research into the Muslim practice of 'zakat'.

Teachers should make use of such activities when beginning work on a particular concept or issue. A series of these activities can be designed, for example, to find out more about the sources or practices relating to the concept. In the case of issues of belief and morality, activities can be directed towards identifying viewpoints and expressing opinions.

Before students can make the most of these activities and achieve as much as they can, the teacher will need to consider the need for careful structuring. After all, students will come to these activities with different stocks of the necessary skills. This will be particularly important at the beginning of a course or stage of schooling where perhaps unfamiliar methods are being introduced. Suppose students are about to begin an investigation into different views about life beyond death. Some students will be able to find relevant material fairly quickly from their school or departmental libraries and make copious and relevant notes. Some will find several books but will have difficulty extracting the relevant information. Others will be struggling to find suitable information since they are unaware of the advantages of an index, even after an appropriate book has been pointed out to them. Thus some form of structure is required within this activity to make it accessible to all students, setting out the various stages and helping them to develop the skills of planning and carrying out an investigation. As the course proceeds, it might be possible to reduce some of the 'props' or introduce a form of differentiation based on differing degrees of help.

Differentiated activities

We saw earlier how 'extension' material is usually understood as work designed to stretch students beyond the level of the core. We saw that one of the disadvantages was that the opportunity to tackle extension or 'enrichment' work depended entirely on passing the core work. Furthermore this depended on how difficult or otherwise students found the core, not to mention how well it was taught. For some students this might mean missing out on the chance to follow up on something that really interested them, or obtain the satisfaction of completing the core work and moving on. All this conjures up a picture of some students continually having difficulty with the core, never able to finish what is known to be the easiest work, condemned for the duration to 'life-on-the-core'. This is clearly unsatisfactory. A better approach would be to introduce a category of **'differentiated activities'**. In this case it will be the activities themselves which are differentiated, in contrast to the open activities where the differentiation is by outcome. For example:

- a group of students are presented with the issue, Is abortion right or wrong and several sources. They are asked to record in their own words information and viewpoints on the issue, give their own opinion and support it with one or two reasons.
- several students complete a piece of extended writing on the issue, 'Reasons for and against belief in God'. They are given a quotation relating to the 'Design' argument, and asked how far such an argument can provide adequate reason for believing in God.

Differentiated activities or tasks can be more consistently applied if they are written according to stated criteria, reflecting different levels of difficulty. As we have seen, Standard Grade Religious Studies has three levels of criteria, Foundation, General and Credit. Any task making demands on students required by a particular level will be differentiated according to that level. For example only at Credit level are students required to know and understand the different ways in which key concepts are interpreted within a community of faith. So a specific task in which students are expected to explain the different ways in which Torah is understood within Jewish tradition would be a Credit level differentiated task. This is likely to be one of a series of tasks making up a differentiated activity or worksheet which only some students would tackle. Some tasks may be suitable for more than one level. For example only at General and Credit levels are students expected to explain the relationship between a religious practice and a related concept. So a specific task where students are asked to explain how Jews' celebration of Passover expresses their belief in salvation, will be a task appropriate for both General and Credit.

As a complement to open activities, tasks and assignments reflecting increasing degrees of difficulty can make a significant contribution towards raising the levels of performance of all students. Since individuals and groups will inevitably complete some open activities at different times, differentiated activities can be introduced to fill the gaps. These will serve either to reinforce learning or develop further skills already acquired. Also, with open activities it seems unlikely that students will always work to the highest possible level of which they are capable. Differentiated tasks provide a means of encouraging students to give of their best. The level of task most appropriate for each individual can be determined on the basis of their performance in open activities. If we are to leave open the possibility that students can improve on what they have done previously, it will be important that they always have the opportunity to attempt tasks at different levels, Finally there is much to be said for informing students about how they can better their performances. Armed with the knowledge of what has to be done in order to improve, there is a much greater chance of them succeeding in doing just that.

NOTES AND BIBLIOGRAPHY

1 Quoted in Sydney Wood *The Shaping of 19th Century Aberdeenshire* Spa Books, 1985, p162
2 ibid. p164
3 Scottish Education Department, Learning and Teaching in Scottish Secondary Schools, Contribution of Eduacational Technology, HMSO, 1982, para.1.1
4 E.C. Wragg, ed. *Classroom Teaching Skills* Croom Helm, 1984
5 ibid. p164
6 John Powell, *Ways of Teaching* Scottish Council for Research in Education, 1985, p8
7 ibid. p9
8 Michael Oakshott, *Learning and Teaching*
9 ibid.
10 Scottish Education Department, *Learning and Teaching in Religious Education* HMSO, 1986, para.4.20
11 Noel Entwistle *Styles of Learning and Teaching* Wiley and Sons, 1981, p26
12 Consultative Council on the Curriculum, Education 10-14, in Scotland, 1986, para.5.29
13 see Chapter 4, Teaching for Personal Development
14 'Learning and Teaching: The Environment and the Primary School Curriculum', HMSO, 1984
15 For example, a database for Religious Education, called Newsline, containing material relating to the views of about twenty different religious groups/churches on about fifty different moral and social issues is available from Jordanhill College of Education, Southbrae Drive, Glasgow.
16 Angela Roger 'Think, Write, Learn, Teaching Activities for Classroom Use across the Curriculum', Scottish Council for Research in Education, 1986
17 Jan Nixon, ed. A Teacher's Guide to Action Research, Grant McIntyre, 1981, p46
18 Douglas Barnes, From Communication to Curriculum, Penguin, 1976, p55
19 Powell, op.cit. p6
20 Donna Brandes and Paul Ginnes *A Guide to Student-Centred Learning* Basil Blackwell, 1986, p33
21 Caroline Cox and John Marks, *Choosing a State School* Century and Hutchison, 1989

4 TEACHING FOR PERSONAL DEVELOPMENT

Looks at how concern for personal development has grown in education by referring to major curriculum papers in both England and Scotland. There is a discussion of several important writers who regard the search for meaning and value as crucial for personal development. The view is expressed that personal development within the curriculum is best thought of in terms of 'process'. The contribution of Religious Education is then described.

PERSONAL DEVELOPMENT IN EDUCATION

In a recent survey of schools H.M. Inspectorate reported that almost all schools had written statements of aims making reference to students' personal development and social education.[1] Although these schools made special mention of the role of guidance staff in this process, they also stressed the responsibility of all teachers for the personal and social development of students.

Education's concern for personal development goes back at least as far as the 1940's. At that time this concern was firmly rooted in the ideal of Christian education. Reporting to the then Secretary of State, the Advisory Council on Education in Scotland insisted that Christian education "means more than finding a place in the curriculum for religious and moral instruction... It involves acceptance of a doctrine of human nature... which will determine the priority of aim in education... It must enter into all debate on the content of schooling; and above all it decisively establishes the child as an end in himself, requiring an approach to him which is patient, persuasive, and at every point respectful of his growth towards personality."[2] The chief end of education, according to the report, is to foster the full and harmonious development of the individual. "The stress we have laid on religion in report after report clearly implies a general acceptance of the great tradition of Christian theism as regulative for our national life and education."[3] A similar position was adopted in England by those who put together the first Agreed Syllabuses in the aftermath of the 1944 Education Act. Few questioned the assumption that the aims of religious education should be directed towards commitment in the Christian religion. Compulsory worship and religious instruction were seen by the Christian denominations as part of the reward for relinquishing control of many church schools to the local authorities. Although it seems that the Act itself was not "a charter for any one view of religious education but for the achievement of a consensus view within each local authority area."[4]

Developments in Scotland

By 1965, when the influential 'Primary Education in Scotland' was published, the dominance of Christianity as the basis for personal development had all but disappeared. Indeed this report was notable for its lack of reference to any kind of religious education. According to its authors, however, this was due to a feeling of inadequacy on their part rather than to any suggestion that the subject was inappropriate to the primary curriculum. The same could not be said for personal development which, although now divorced from religion, was given a vital role within the aims of education. It was essential, said the report, to satisfy the needs of the individual for growth and development as well as paying attention to the demands and expectations of society. More than ever before, the report claimed, primary schools had to concern themselves with the emotional and social development of their students. It quoted with approval the Schools (Scotland) Code which emphasised the importance of cultivating "the qualities of truthfulness, honesty, self-control and consideration for man and beast... and to develop a sense of responsibility to the community and an attitude of good-will towards other peoples." And in a significant statement the report continued, "It cannot be too strongly stressed that education is concerned as much with the personal development of the child as with the teaching of subjects."[5]

More than a decade later the Munn Report was published revealing the same concern for the needs of the individual. It was important that the curriculum be responsive to the needs of society, said Munn, "but it must be equally sensitive to the needs of individual pupils, helping them to make sense of their personal circumstances, preparing them for adult life, and enriching their experience as individuals."[6] The report identified four sets of aims for secondary schools each of which contained a specific concern for students' personal and social development. Within the first set of aims relating to the development of knowledge and understanding the report makes mention of the self as well as of the social and physical environment. Schools are asked to ensure that students are given the opportunity to explore "the world of subjective experience" and to contribute to their "physical, mental and spiritual well-being".[7] The second set of aims is concerned with skills, particularly interpersonal skills. Among these it identified the ability to get on with others, to express sympathy and to behave appropriately in groups, discussions and other social situations. The third set of aims looks to the affective development of students. Here the report is referring to the emotional and moral development of students and the encouragement positive attitudes and values. In particular it draws attention to such qualities as concern for others and openness to change, and to values such as tolerance, fairness and respect for evidence. The fourth set of aims is concerned with the demands of society including those aspects of knowledge and skills which relate to personal relationships and family life.

In an important recent document addressed particularly to Headteachers and their senior staff, the Scottish Consultative Council on the Curriculum has attempted to describe how schools might implement goals relating to personal and social development. Essential to every student's personal and social development, they argue, is a number of key process skills and elements. These key skills and elements are said to be "part of the climate in which the learning takes place" and therefore permeate the whole curriculum.[8] Sometimes they will appear as part of established courses and sometimes as courses in their own right. It is the responsibility of all teachers to ensure that these skills and elements form part of every student's education. Among the process skills are accessing information, learning strategies, communication skills as well as critical thinking and problem solving. Included in the key elements are health, rights and responsibilities, tolerance, care of the environment and personal guidance. As a primary means of delivering these the document emphasises the importance of teaching methods and the nature of students' learning experiences. Process skills and elements of personal development are to be acquired most effectively through the use of discursive, enquiry and other activity approaches. In addition, subject departments are to incorporate into their established syllabuses components which are designed to contribute specifically to the development of process skills and elements of personal and social development. Specially devised courses may also be on offer as part of a personal and social education programme or in the form of 40 hour short courses and modules for students in the 14-18 age group.

Both the process skills and the elements of personal and social development above include components which are relatively new additions to the curriculum. They result from the perceived needs of a rapidly changing society and changing views about the nature of knowledge.[9] Whether they together constitute an adequate description of personal development seems to me doubtful. Some curricular areas and subjects may be seen as making their own contribution to personal and social development, and not just through the components stated above. I want to suggest in this chapter that religious education in particular contributes in a very significant way to this area of the curriculum. This point, I think, emerges much more clearly within developments currently taking place in England.

Developments in England

In England, HMI reports and DES publications have been taking up the theme of personal and social development. 'Education in Schools', for example, which set out general aims, included among these the importance of "helping children develop lively, enquiring minds; giving them the ability to question and to argue rationally," and instilling "respect for moral values... and tolerance of other races, religions, and ways of life."[10] 'Curriculum 11-16' stressed the importance of schools helping students to acquire a basic understanding of themselves and of the society in which they live. Skills of communication, discussion, of independent learning and of cooperation with others were highlighted. Students need to be able to discriminate between fact and fiction, between reasoned argument and prejudice "so that they feel confident in making choices and decisions."[11]

Some reports have seen a special place for religious education within personal and social development. The HMI report, 'A View of the Curriculum' declared, "schools need to secure for all pupils opportunities for learning particularly likely to contribute to personal and social development. Religious education clearly has a contribution to make here" as well as a "study of personal relationships, moral education and health education."[12] The Schools Council's 'Primary Practice', identified four main aspects of this area of the curriculum. These were personal qualities, relationships with other people, religious education and moral education. Among the personal qualities the report has in mind are a sense of self respect, independence and the ability to question and argue rationally. As far as developing the ability to relate to others is concerned, creating the right environment within which "politeness, empathy, social competence and helpfulness can flourish is the key task."[13] Children need practice at working as members of a group, contributing to group discussions, accepting leadership roles and learning to accommodate the views of other people.

In 1981 the Assessment of Performance Unit published a document called 'Personal and Social Development'. The Unit had been set up by the DES in 1975 to provide information about standards and levels of performance across the curriculum. Although they could find "no satisfactory way round the difficulties inherent" in assessing personal and social development, they felt that a careful definition of the content and skills involved would be of interest to educators.[14] They suggested that personal and social development could be broken down into a series of aspects. These were first, aspects of general development, such as personal relationships, morality and social awareness; and second, aspects of specific development, such as careers, health, the environment and community involvement. In addition they identified religion and philosophies of life as being important but were unable to decide whether they belonged in the general or the specific category. They concluded:

"Religion and philosophies of life posed a problem. This area can be seen as fundamental and all-pervasive; the key to all personal and social development. Alternatively, religious knowledge and understanding can be seen to be at least as specific as knowing about careers or understanding the environment. A compromise was made and the area dealt with separately."[15]

Within the National Curriculum the personal and social development of students is a major aim. Circular number six stated that the ten core and foundation subjects of the national curriculum were not intended to be the whole of the curriculum. In addition, provision must be made for cross-curricular elements which are concerned with "the intentional promotion of personal and social development through the curriculum as a whole."[16] These were identified as dimensions, skills and themes:

- dimensions comprise a commitment to provide equal opportunities for all students and the introduction of multi-cultural perspectives. These enable students to view the world from different standpoints and to develop an attitude of open-mindedness. Also consideration must be given on an individual basis to meeting the requirements of students with special educational needs.
- skills such as communication skills, numeracy, problem solving, study skills and skills of a personal and social nature, should be developed throughout the curriculum and in a variety of contexts.
- themes, which are to have a strong component of knowledge and understanding as well as skills, are said to be essential parts of the whole curriculum. They are, economic and industrial understanding, careers education and guidance, health education, education for citizenship, environmental education. Each of the themes is to feature somewhere in the curriculum. In primary schools they might be included in a topic approach, while in secondary they might be separately timetabled or subsumed within existing subjects.

Although all the curricular elements above contribute significantly to personal and social development they do not, say the NCC, encompass all that is personal and social education. "...subjects of the National Curriculum, religious education, additional subjects and extra-curricular activities... also play their part."[17]

PERSONAL DEVELOPMENT: A PSYCHOLOGICAL PERSPECTIVE

In his book on personal and social education Richard Pring reviews the contribution of a number of writers to the concept of personal development.[18] He examines Piaget's view that morality is basically a system of rules for which the individual must acquire respect. He surveys the work of Lawrence Kohlberg who has investigated the structure of young people's thinking about moral issues. He outlines the stages of role-taking which Robert Selman believes explains the development of a person's ability to appreciate a point of view different from one's own. And he describes the theory of Jane Loevinger who attempts to set out a more comprehensive account of the development of the person.

Although Pring's analysis is helpful in alerting us to dominant themes within the notion of personal development, it is noticeable for what it omits, namely, any reference to the place of religious or spiritual development. I for one find it difficult to imagine how any concept of personal development can hold its own without some such reference to people's concern for meaning and purpose. As Michael Grimmitt has recently reminded us, "implicit in each religion's understanding of the religious or spiritual quest is its understanding of the meaning and end of personal development."[19] To supplement Pring's analysis I want to look at the work of a number of writers who regard the search for meaning as an essential element in personal development.

Most students of religion are familiar with aspects of the work of the great psychoanalyst, Sigmund Freud. In his book 'The Future of an Illusion' Freud interpreted religion as the individual's flight from the frustrations of life towards the illusion of belief in a divine father. His studies made him very sensitive to the abuses of religious faith frequently found in neurotic individuals. Those psychologists and psychoanalysts, however, who have devoted their attention to the study of healthy individuals have come to very different conclusions. They tend to see the possession of a religious outlook on life as a positive force contributing to personal maturity. Among these are Carl Jung, Gordon Allport, Erich Fromm and James Fowler.

Carl Jung

For much of his work Carl Jung was not so much interested in the relationships between people as in the changes which were going on inside individuals. He saw the mind as a self-regulating organism requiring a continuous balancing of opposites for the maintenance of health. It was crucial according to Jung that a person accept his or her darker side with all its irrational, meaningless and even evil elements. In his treatment of patients

Jung was very concerned to encourage the use of imagination through writing, modelling and painting. Through this Jung believed people could be put in touch with the better side of themselves and so begin the self-regulating process.

One of the significant features of Jung's patients was that in general they did not suffer from any ordinary type of neurosis but instead had fallen victim to "the senselessness and aimlessness of their lives."[20] What required to be solved was precisely this lack of sense and direction in the patient's life. For Jung the cure was related to questions about the meaning of life. What will the doctor do, he observed, when he discovers the causes of his patient's illness, when he discovers that his patient has, "no faith, because he is afraid to grope in the dark; no hope, because he is disillusioned by the world and by life; and no understanding, because he has failed to read the meaning of his own existence."[21] For Freud religion produces neurosis but for Jung religion can effect the cure and prevent its rise. By religion Jung did not have in mind any particular belief system, but rather the general search for a pattern of meaning and value by which to live. In his experience some pattern of meaning and value was the key to healthy growth and development. He wrote:

"Among all my patients in the second half of life - that is to say, over thirty five - there has not been one whose problem in the last resort was not that of finding a religious outlook on life. It is safe to say that every one of them fell ill because they had lost what the living religions of every age have given to their followers, and none of them has been really healed who did not regain his religious outlook. This, of course, has nothing to do with a particular creed or membership of a church."[22]

It was during his work with such patients that Jung began to formulate his theory of individuation. In broad terms individuation is concerned with a person's effort to become whole. It means coming to terms with oneself through reconciling the various sides of one's personality. It is about coming to grips with the darker side of one's nature, and establishing who we are over against the various roles we have in life. It is a process sometimes referred to as "self-actualisation or self-realisation or even the attainment of maturity."[23] It was Jung's view that religions and quasi-religions can play an important part in this process of becoming. Creeds, moral codes and rituals can all provide opportunities for expressing deep and often unconscious needs relating to our identity, relationships and the search for meaning. Although Jung saw religion as a valuable element in the achievement of an integrated personality, he was himself always agnostic about the objective or metaphysical truth of religious beliefs. As a student of psychology and religion he was only interested in what human beings had thought and done about religion, not in its truth or falsity."What makes his thought interesting," says Don Cupitt, "is that he fully accepts the projection-theory of religion developed by atheists like Feuerbach and Marx, and then unexpectedly turns it around and derives from it a new set of arguments for taking religion very seriously indeed."[24]

G.W. Allport

The Harvard psychologist, G.W. Allport, has devoted his research and writing to the study of the healthy and mature human personality. He claims to take a total view of the human person with a range of factors within heredity and environment influencing the kind of person we become. For Allport one of the most striking phenomena of the developing person is our continuing sense of self-identity, even though every other aspect of our personality will have changed over the years. He points particularly to the importance of our own name. By hearing our own name repeatedly as children we gradually see ourselves as distinct and separate from things around us.

Like many other writers in this field Allport points to the search for self-identity as a key feature also of adolescence. The basis of the identity problem for the adolescent says Allport is the choosing of an occupation or other life goal. For the adolescent it is vital to establish some kind of plan for the future "and in this respect his sense of selfhood takes on a dimension entirely lacking in childhood."[25] The adolescent begins to take on a number of long range purposes and distant goals which edge him into adulthood. Admittedly some of these may be too ambitious and idealistic and will be pared down in the years to come. Allport remarks, "It is not necessary that the goals be rigidly focussed, but only that a central theme of striving be present."[26]

When he turns his attention to the qualities most characteristic of the mature person, Allport picks out three in particular. The first of these is 'self-extension'. This is the ability to place our energies and interests outside ourselves, to set aside self-interest and attend to a cause or value which extends beyond our immediate sphere of operation. The second quality is the 'ability to be objective' about ourselves. Accurate self-knowledge, says Allport, is not easy to achieve. Most people think they know themselves well. If we wish to find out the degree of a person's self knowledge we really need to measure what a person thinks he is like in relation to what others think he is like. People with a high level of insight, says Allport, tend to be better judges of other people and consequently are more likely to be accepted by them. Also people with good insight who are aware of their bad points are less likely to project them on to others. The third quality is the possession of a 'unifying philosophy of life'. The person who has achieved this will have "a clear comprehension of life's purpose in terms of an intelligible theory."[27] He or she will have achieved some synthesis of the vast collection of loosely related thoughts and feelings which comprise our individuality. He or she will have gained some resolution of the conflicting ideals and viewpoints which arise within our personal and social relations. All this will be held together not necessarily comfortably but perhaps in some kind of tension within a meaningful framework of beliefs and values. As for religion, claims Allport, it is ideally designed to be the source of such personal unity. After all, religion encompasses "all that lies within experience and all that lies beyond... But the fact remains that many people find a high degree of unification in other directions."[28]

Erich Fromm

For Erich Fromm the religious outlook is rooted firmly in the basic conditions of human existence. Two characteristics, he argues, combined to produce it. First, human beings evolved with a minimum capacity for determining their behaviour through instinct. Second, they emerged with a brain capacity far in excess of any previous species. Without the ability to act by instinct and at the same time possessing the ability to reason, reflect and imagine, the human species, needed a 'frame of orientation' and an 'object of devotion' in order to survive. By 'object of devotion' Fromm does not necessarily have in mind any concept of God, but rather "a focal point for all our strivings and a basis for all our... values."[29] We need this, argues Fromm, in order to transcend our essentially isolated existence, filled with doubts and uncertainties, and to satisfy our need for a meaning to life. Human beings would be confused and insecure without a frame of reference or overall picture of the world to share with those around them. It is a fact, states Fromm, that no culture has ever been found which did not have such a frame of reference. Although individuals often claim not to possess any overall picture giving direction to their life, "it can be easily demonstrated that they simply take their own philosophy for granted because to them it is only common sense."[30] Moreover, according to Fromm, it does not matter much whether our overall philosophy of life is true or false, as long as it fulfils its psychological function, of enabling us to live a purposeful life and establish values which can form the basis of our relationships with others.

James Fowler

No investigation into personal development today can afford to overlook the work of James Fowler. His theory of 'faith development' first emerged during 1968 and 1969 while he was working for a religious and cultural centre in North Carolina called Interpreter's House. As a counsellor he became involved in listening to dozens of life histories. Gradually he began to perceive patterns and common features among the widely differing relationships and events that made up peoples' lives. A year later while teaching graduate students at Harvard Divinity School, "the outlines of a broad developmental approach to faith began to take shape."[31] It was not until 1981 that his most complete study based on nearly 400 interviews appeared under the title "Stages of Faith: The Psychology of Human Development and the Quest for Meaning."

One of the most distinctive features of his research and one which gives it great value as far as religious education is concerned is the broad significance he attaches to the word 'faith'. This enables him to include illustrations from religious and non-religious people. For Fowler faith is a way of knowing or interpreting experience. It represents the core of a person, colouring and shaping his or her most fundamental attitudes to life, death and relationships. Through the activity of forming faith a person finds meaning and establishes some priority of values. For Fowler faith is first and foremost a human phenomenon, expressing a universal tendency among people to search for meaning and provide coherence to life.

> "Prior to our being religious or irreligious, before we come to think of ourselves as Catholics, Protestants, Jews or Muslims, we are already engaged with issues of faith. Whether we become non-believers, agnostics or atheists, we are concerned with how to put our lives together and with what will make life worth living."[32]

Fowler's research suggests that there are six recognisable and distinct stages in a person's capacity to develop meaning and value in life. Each stage is structurally complete in itself but is linked to the next stage hierarchically. Stage one is followed by stage two and so on. Fowler outlines a number of specific abilities which shape the nature of faith at each stage. These are logical thinking, moral judgement, ability to take on roles, interpreting symbols, social awareness, and the ability to unify meanings. These abilities which Fowler considers to be part of a person's capacity for faith are so broad that his description of faith development amounts to a description of the development of the whole person.[33]

Fowler calls his first stage **Intuitive-Projective**. In this stage, the child, whose age ranges from two or three to six or seven, uses the new tools of speech and symbolic representation to organise his or her experience and to make meanings. With words and names the child explores, orders and sorts out the unknown world. From a cognitive perspective the child's thinking lacks logical sequence. It is episodic with associations flowing according to the processes of the imagination. Knowing is primarily by intuition as the child begins to discover a reality beyond immediate experience, and encounters the limits of life such as death, power, good and evil. Trust is grounded in parents and other significant adults, and the world is known by intuitively projecting meaning in imitation of those adults (hence the name of the stage, intuitive-projective). Fact and fantasy intertwined and symbols are taken literally. The capacity to take the role of the other is just beginning.

The particular focus of this stage is the emergence of 'imagination', enabling the child to come to terms with the world of experience through engagement with a variety of images and symbols. For this stage, Fowler stresses the importance of fairy tales and of many biblical narratives. These, he says, provide a way for children to represent their inner feelings and to find appropriate images and symbols by which they can begin to shape their lives. By being immersed in stories of all kinds, children can begin to develop and express their intuitive understandings and feelings about themselves, their immediate relationships and elements of the natural world.

Whereas the Intuitive-Projective child makes no distinction between fantasy, fact and feeling, the **Mythic-Literal** child of stage 2 works hard and effectively at sorting out the real from the unreal. This stage coincides with the onset of concrete operations in which the child is capable of a step-by-step form of logical reasoning and of seeing the relation between cause and effect. The child is able to reverse operations. He or she can move forward or backward, and see that the parts explain the whole, or that the whole is constituted by the parts. In addition, the child at this stage is capable of a whole new level of projection and anticipation of consequences. As long as it is a concrete situation the child is addressing, he or she can look ahead, anticipate the results and make forecasts about the outcome. This ability to look ahead and anticipate outcomes, together with the expanded ability for logical reasoning is linked to the child's emerging capacity for critical reflection. I shall take up this point again in chapter six.

The particular focus of stage 2 as far as faith development is concerned, is the emergence of story and myth as ways of finding meaning in experience. These are taken literally (hence the stage's name, mythic-literal). Younger children depend upon stories to provide images and symbols for the strong feelings and impulses forming within them. But they do not yet generate stories. The new elements within concrete operational thinking described above furnish the means by which children can retell the stories they are told and make them their own. The capacity for, and interest in narrative makes the Mythic-Literal child particularly attentive to the stories that are associated with the family and community to which he or she belongs. Stories of lives and of great adventures, true or fictional, appeal to them, and extend their experience and understanding of life. Stage 2 children, however, have not yet developed the ability to step back from stories, reflect upon them, and communicate their meanings by way of more abstract and general statements. The meanings remain to a large extent within the narrative, since there is not yet a readiness to draw from them any general conclusions about meaning and value in life.

In Fowler's stage 3, which begins about age twelve, a person's experience of the world is extending well beyond the family, into school or work, peers and perhaps religion. Although typically this stage begins in adolescence it becomes permanent for many adults. In the main a person's outlook or view of life follows the conventions of others, conforming to the judgements and expectations of those outside himself including sources of authority. At this stage, however, a person does not have sufficient grasp of his own identity or possess autonomous judgement to follow through an independent line. The person's ideology consists of a cluster of beliefs and values which more or less hang together, but which have not yet been subject to critical examination.

One of the clearest examples of stage 3 was a truck driver whose personal philosophy of life reflected what he saw as the views of 'the man in the street'. He tended to dismiss any questions about the purpose of human life as being essentially meaningless and incomprehensible. Yet he does present the outlines of a view of the meaning of life, albeit in terms of a loose collection of opinions and convictions, which he identifies as being just common sense. Fowler describes stage 3 as **Synthetic/Conventional**. Conventional because the individual sees his or her faith as being everybody's faith, the faith of the community, however that is perceived. Synthetic because it is essentially non-analytical. The truck driver talks about the values involved not in order to distinguish his own views, or hold them up for examination, but in order to establish common ground with the community of which he feels a part. Summing up his view of life, he declares,

> "I'm not now a religious man, never was, and never will be. Religion is just a lot of nonsense as I see it. As I see it, we are born, we live here, we die, and that's it. Religion gives people something more, because they want there to be something more, but there isn't."[34]

In a similar example of Stage 3 faith, fifteen year old Linda talks about her beliefs, this time from within a church community which appears to set definite limits to questions about belief. When asked what she meant by 'going to heaven' she replied,

> "Well, nobody really knows. It's supposed to be Paradise. And, I guess I'll find out sometime. But, see, I don't want to ask too many questions like that. I always want to... well, lots of people have really done research on religion and they've gone insane, you know? I've never wanted to go that much into it. I just want to do what the Bible says."[35]

Stage 4 is called by Fowler **Individuative/Reflective**. This terminology signals an important transition away from a faith accepted from others solely on their authority, towards a more personal faith resulting from re-examination of long held beliefs. The ideas of others are less likely to be accepted uncritically and more attention will be given to expressing and justifying personal opinions. Fowler suggests that this stage begins in mid or late adolescence, although it may not occur until well into adult life. It is not unusual, says Fowler, for a Stage 4 person to join a strong ideological community offering ready made answers to the ambiguities and paradoxes in life. The tendency, however, is for them to take an either/or approach to such questions. Nevertheless the new ability to stand alone means that any group or community is chosen after reflection rather than simply accepted or received.

In Stage 5, the person shows a willingness to live with ambiguity and shades of grey. He or she exhibits genuine openness to the opinions of others even at the risk of having to change his or her own views, recognising that one's own position does not represent the final fullness of truth. There is present an active concern for all peoples and groups and not just for one's own immediate community. The strength of this stage, says Fowler, is "a capacity to see and be in one's group's most powerful meanings, while simultaneously recognising that they are relative, partial and inevitably distorting apprehensions of transcendent reality."[36]

Fowler insists that each stage has an integrity of its own. His first and second stages, however, are essentially childhood phases, whereas the third and fourth, while beginning in adolescence, can become permanent homes for many adults. A person can live quite happily at any of stages 3, 4, or 5, provided nothing happens to disturb the equilibrium. For example, clashes between sources of parental or religious authority, and newly encountered viewpoints in Stage 3, can lead to radical questioning of one's own position and transition to Stage 4. Stage four is not better than stage three, rather it is a more developed and mature expression of faith than stage three, each representing a different plateau of understanding, feelings and judgement in relation to a person's experiences and sphere of operation. Each stage of development, therefore, has its own particular pattern of meaning and value, although the content of such a 'faith' may differ markedly within each stage. At each stage the pattern of meaning and value has a different focus. In Stage 3 it focusses on the desire to be one with the community; in Stage 4 the focus is the independent self; while in Stage 5 there is a universal dimension not present at earlier stages.

Personal Development and Religious Education

In his recent book Michael Grimmitt provides us with a powerful treatment of the way in which religious education contributes to personal development. The contribution of religious education, and indeed of education generally, requires says Grimmitt the development of self-knowledge in students. "The process of becoming 'self-aware' (which culminates in self-knowledge) involves our becoming conscious of those beliefs and values which have shaped us as a person, and more particularly, have formed our identity."[37] So how is this self-knowledge to be developed according to Grimmitt? First, by encouraging students to reflect on dilemmas and questions which arise either within their own lives or in the lives of others. Questions, for example, which arise from the death of a relative or friend, or the failure of a personal relationship. These should lead to a process of reflection on one's own beliefs and values. This process of reflection, remarks Grimmitt, is the means by which we become self-aware. Second, through the study of religions students can be helped to understand not only the importance of beliefs and values for others, but also how these can contribute to their own self-understanding.

Becoming conscious of our own beliefs and values, particularly those which have shaped us as persons, is, Grimmitt admits, a complex process. It is not just a matter of becoming aware of their content, but more especially of examining them and exercising an informed choice "between them and between other beliefs and values which may be available to us."[38] An essential element in this process is the application of certain skills, particularly those skills relating to the realm of critical thinking and evaluation. Although Grimmitt does acknowledge the crucial part to be played by 'evaluation' in the process of acquiring self-knowledge, he has little specifically to say about what students will actually be doing when they evaluate and in what activities teachers might engage them in order to help them do it better.

His distinction between personal and impersonal evaluation, although a helpful one in terms of analysis of the processes involved, is likely to be less clear in practice. When asked, for example, to evaluate the Hindu belief in reincarnation, students may proceed by asking whether or not they find it at all persuasive (personal evaluation). They may justify their position in terms of whether it accords with their own experience of life so far. But they are just as likely to justify their opinion using criteria which could be categorised as psychological, philosophical or even theological (impersonal evaluation). As Grimmitt explains these are essentially "alternative interpretations, differing from an adherent's understanding of his or her faith."[39] Indeed the first may well involve elements from the second. Student responses most of the time therefore are likely to be as much personal evaluations as impersonal ones. Even in the realm of religious practices, where students may be asked to consider the value of the Hajj for the lives of individual Muslims and the Muslim community, students may well respond in ways that reveal its attractiveness for themselves.

Grimmitt's curriculum illustrations, which form part two of his book, are particularly useful with regard to what he calls 'learning from religion'. It is within these sections that issues are raised and opportunities for evaluation highlighted. If we are to help students to take advantage of these suggestions, we need to be much clearer about what skills are involved and how we can encourage their effective development. I have tried to do this in my chapter on evaluation. Since Grimmitt's illustrations are mainly 'content' illustrations, attention is inevitably drawn to the importance of choosing content appropriate to the promotion of self-knowledge. It is equally important, if not more so, to devise appropriate, in the sense of 'active', learning experiences. These should provide students with successive opportunities to practise essential skills. It is my experience that if teachers are not convinced and enthusiastic about the importance of 'active' learning, then it is unlikely that students will develop much in the way of self-knowledge, however appropriate the content. Although they may for all that learn a great deal about religion.

Grimmitt's study serves to remind us, in a most scholarly way, that it is not knowledge of things primarily which makes for personal development but knowledge of ourselves. This 'personal knowledge' is acquired by applying formal knowledge to our own concerns. It is the result of interaction between the formal knowledge of say religions, politics, the environment, the physical world, and our own ideas about what it means to be human. It is therefore, first and foremost, a matter of process or rather several processes. Philip Phenix, in his discussion of personal knowledge, points to a number of features which serve to distinguish it from formal knowledge and at the same time confirm our view of it as 'process'. Within formal knowledge, writes Phenix, the knower stands apart from what he knows, he is detached from the subject matter. The acquisition of personal knowledge on the other hand requires engagement with what is to be learned, the knowledge is subjective and insights concern the self or relationships involving the self. Personal knowledge is not for the most part developed through instruction. It is the result primarily of normal human relating within families, between friends, and at school or work.[40] Within classrooms it will depend on the use made of group methods and discursive activities, as well as the relationships fostered between teacher and students.

Personal development as process

Personal knowledge then is at the root of personal development, and is the result of being involved in certain processes. I want to suggest that personal development is best thought of in terms of four interrelated processes. These are directed towards developing in students the capacity for:

(a) exercising autonomy
(b) relating appropriately to individuals and within groups
(c) responsible moral actions
(d) finding meaning and value in life

(a) exercising autonomy

Autonomy consists in the development of such abilities as choosing, deciding, reflecting, planning and judging. Although it is most often used in connection with moral education, it is applicable in any area where a person intends to give reasons for what he or she thinks and does. It can be exercised within the field of political judgements, in choosing a job, planning a holiday, and deciding whether we believe in God. R.F. Dearden explains: "A person is autonomous to the degree, and it is very much a matter of degree, that what he thinks and does at least in important areas of his life, are determined by himself."[41] The exercise of such autonomy is likely to be the source of considerable personal satisfaction. To see our plans and intentions coming to fruition through our own efforts is to obtain a sense of achievement, which contributes to our sense of personal worth, vital for healthy personal development.

In religious education we can contribute to young people's growing sense of autonomy by helping them to decide for themselves what to believe. This requires in particular, developing the ability to handle issues of belief and morality effectively and with sensitivity. It means encouraging students to apply appropriate questions as part of the task of understanding and evaluating issues. In relation to issues of belief, for example, the following questions will be important:

- What evidence is there to support the belief?
- Is there any contradictory evidence and how important is it?
- How far does it contribute to my own search for meaning?

In relation to an issue of morality we might ask:

- Have I taken into account all the factors?
- What principles or values are involved?
- Are there any relevant teachings within religious traditions and their sacred writings?
- What alternative viewpoints are there?

But however important we consider autonomy to be it is clearly not the only thing that matters. Without a developed sense of morality, for example, the autonomous person is likely to be a malign influence, leading himself and others into successive misadventures with perhaps calamitous results. "Great criminals," Dearden notes, "are markedly autonomous men."[42] There will also be a tendency to exaggerate the idea of individualism as the foundation of autonomy and to ignore the social context of our development as individuals. Autonomy therefore must be complemented by a sense of responsibility and an ability to relate to others.

(b) relating appropriately to individuals and within groups

The ability to see oneself and others as persons is an essential characteristic of being a person. This ability to see that others too have certain feelings, thoughts and motives, and that this has implications for my relationships with them is something which grows only gradually. Young children do not at first realise that other people's feelings and intentions may be different from their own. Witness the three year old as he tries to attract a parent's attention completely ignoring any activity in which the parent may be engaged at that precise moment. My own son, I recall, developed the irritating habit of grasping my bearded chin and turning my head until it faced the right direction. Many, though, reach the stage of realising that other people's feelings and preoccupations may be different from their own, and in the process acquire an idea of what it means to be a person, yet fail to apply it very widely. Pring writes:

> "Different periods of history show how the concept of person was not applied to particular people - to blacks, or to heathens, or to slaves, or to women, or to children."[43]

The context for much of this kind of work in religious education will be the beliefs and values of a variety of religious traditions both inside and outside mainland Britain. Although discussion will be directed towards promoting knowledge and understanding of how others live and view the world, a central aim will be to help students to stand in other people's shoes, to see things from someone else's point of view. Young people will face difficulties in learning to consider other people's interests and feelings. This kind of empathic study of religion, learning to accept and respect differences, can make an important contribution to students' ability to relate to others.

(c) responsible moral actions
The process of developing persons capable of responsible moral actions is usually called moral education. As I have already remarked, being a person involves centrally the capacity to enter into relationship with others. Inevitably choices and decisions will often have to be made. Our actions will be open to the judgement of others regarding their motives and consequences. The basis of such judgements is likely to be those values and principles which attract a broad consensus, for example fairness and justice, freedom, consideration for the interests of others, and the importance of telling the truth. There is more to developing the capability for moral actions, however, than knowing the rules and principles involved. Young people need to develop the skills required for making relevant judgements, as well as the much more difficult quality of motivation for putting them into practice. This was very much the focus of the 'Lifeline' material which sought to develop in young people a 'considerate style of life', by placing their own feelings and concerns at the centre of classroom activities.[44] I take up the subject of moral education again in the next chapter.

(d) finding meaning and value in life

It has been customary in recent years to think of religious education as being concerned with students' search for meaning, value and purpose in life. John Hull, however, has rightly drawn our attention to the weaknesses of this view. One is "that it claims for religious education something which is really the task of the whole curriculum."[45] We have already seen how Philip Phenix regards the whole of education as being "grounded in the search for meaning." Every subject has the potential for contributing to students' search for meaning in so far as they include discussion of beliefs and values or the concept of truth. Examples might be the relationship between facts and values in the presentation of experimental results in the sciences or the issues of morality that can arise within history or physical education.[46] So what distinctive contribution can the study of religion make to students' search for meaning? Through a planned and systematic programme of activities students can develop the ability to:

- look critically at their own beliefs and values
- express and justify opinions on religious and moral issues
- explain the personal and social implications of adopting particular beliefs and values

These processes are the substance of **learning from religion** and involve exploring the religious and moral dimensions of personal and social development. They are mainly concerned with developing the skills of reflecting and evaluating. Looking critically at our own beliefs and values means not only becoming aware of them but also asking, 'why these beliefs and values?' It involves exploring the roots of our own identity, perhaps resulting, as in Fowler's Stage 3, in the gradual realisation that our tightly held convictions are not so much 'ours' as the community's of which we are a part. This process requires careful and sensitive handling. Much of the outcome will remain and should remain private, inaccessible certainly to the teacher's techniques of assessment. Something of the process, however, may emerge in the opinions which students are being encouraged to justify. Students' responses to a question about the existence of God may reflect a change in their own views or alternatively represent a firmer appreciation of the received consensus of a particular religious community. Both responses would be acceptable provided they went beyond mere affirmation of faith to include valid reasoning. The educator's main concern will be with the quality of this reasoning rather than with any change which may have occurred in students' own beliefs and values. Taken together these abilities require activities which will encourage students to ask questions such as:

What am I really like? How do I feel about myself? How do others see me? How do I feel about others? What kind of person would I like to be?	**Questions of Identity**
How do I act towards others? How do others act towards me? Why do I act towards others like this? What is the right thing for me to do?	**Questions of Relationships**
Why do I believe in this? Why do I regard this as important? Why do I regard this person / group as significant to me? What seems to me to be worth living for? Whom do I admire? What do they believe in? What views about life / themselves do they hold?	**Questions of Meaning**
Are these beliefs / values / practices attractive to me? If I adopted them what difference would it make to my personal life / relationships to others / view of life? Would these beliefs / values be helpful as a guide to my everyday living? Do they help to make sense of human life and human relationships? Are they consistent with what I know about the world from my own experience? What alternative views are there?	**Questions of Judgement**

To persuade pupils to ask such questions of their own beliefs and values may be no easy matter. Some may regard their existing pattern of belief as more than adequate, particularly if it is shared by their parents and supported by a vibrant church community. Others will not be aware of the contradictions between the different beliefs which they hold and will fail to see the need to examine them. It is particularly important therefore that these abilities are developed against a background of understanding of the world's religious and non-religious systems of belief. These provide a context within which students can reflect on their own beliefs in dialogue with the beliefs and values of the religion being studied. The traditional belief systems are particularly appropriate vehicles for this dialogue since they provide "models by which people have been sustained as persons, pursuing purposes beyond their immediate interests, finding meaning to life which includes the other person, and establishing wherein value is to be found."[47] This is the substance of **learning about religion**, involving as it does the exploration of religious beliefs, practices and sources. It will also involve the exploration of the human experiences which ultimately give rise to these; experiences which relate to such things as personal identity, relationships, the natural world, stages of life. Learning about religion will involve asking questions such as:

- What are the central beliefs or key concepts within the religion being studied?
- How are these beliefs expressed within the religion's scriptures and sacred writings?
- What practices can be observed within the religion and how do these relate to the beliefs or key concepts?
- What do the beliefs, concepts or practices contribute to our understanding of the human experiences which underly them?
- What understanding of authority does the religion have and how is it expressed?

NOTES AND BIBLIOGRAPHY

1   *Learning and Teaching in the First Two Years of the Scottish Secondary School*, HMSO, 1986, para.4.1
2   Secondary Education, A Report of the Advisory Council on Education in Scotland, para.28
3   ibid para. 48
4   Dennis Starkings *Approaching World Religions* Oxford, 1982, p63
5   Primary Education in Scotland, 1965, pp36-37
6   The Structure of the Curriculum in the Third and Fourth Years of the Scottish Secondary School (Munn Report) HMSO, 1977 para.3.4
7   ibid para.4.3
8   Curriculum Design for the Secondary Stages, SCCC, 1989, para.3.6
9   see chapter 2
10 Education in Schools, DES, 1977, p6
11 Curriculum 11-16, DES, 1977, p12
12 A View of the Curriculum, HMSO, 1980
13 Schools Council,Primary Practice, Working Paper 75, p93
14 Assessment of Performance Unit, Personal and Social Development, 1981
15 ibid p5
16 Circular Number 6, The National Curriculum and Whole Curriculum Planning: Preliminary Guidance, National Curriculum Council, 1989, para.9
17 Curriculum Guidance 3, The Whole Curriculum, National Curriculum Council, 1990, p7
18 Richard Pring *Personal and Social Education in the Curriculum* Hodder and Stoughton, 1984
19 Michael Grimmitt *Religious Education and Human Development* McCrimmons,1987, p160
20 Anthony Storr *The Dynamics of Creation* Penguin, 1972, p283
21 Carl Jung 'Psychotherapists or the Clergy', in *Psychology and Religion:West and East* Routledge,vol.2, p331
22 ibid p334
23 Anthony Storr, op.cit. p283
24 Don Cupitt *The Sea of Faith* BBC, 1984, p76
25 G.W.Allport *Becoming:Basic Considerations for a Psychology of Personality* Yale, 1955, p126
26 ibid p126
27 ibid p294
28 ibid p302
29 Erich Fromm To *Have or To Be*, Abucus 1979, p138

30 ibid p138
31 James Fowler *Stages of Faith:The Psychology of Human Development and the Quest for Meaning*, Harper and Row, 1981, p38
32 ibid p5
33 Thomas Groome *Christian Religious Education* Harper and Row, 1980, p81
34 Fowler op.cit. p166
35 ibid p157
36 ibid p198
37 Grimmitt op.cit. p157
38 ibid p157
39 ibid p226
40 Philip Phenix *Realms of Meaning* McGraw-Hill, 1964, p193ff

41 R.F.Dearden, 'Autonomy and Education', in *Education and Reason,* ed. Hirst, Peters, Dearden, Routledge, 1972, p71
42 ibid p71
43 Pring op.cit. p18
44 Schools Council Moral Education Project 13-16, Longman, 1972
45 John Hull, British Journal of R.E. Winter 1980, p41
46 see *Values Across the Curriculum* Falmer Press, 1986
47 Bruce Wallace *Personal Development, in Educating for Tomorrow:A Lothian Perspective* Holmes McDougall, 1984, p17

5 RELIGIOUS, MORAL AND SOCIAL EDUCATION

Discusses two major strands within the literature relating to moral education, the consideration of principles and the development of abilities and attitudes. Differing views of social education are looked at in both Scotland and England, and the links between moral and social education are discussed in relation to primary and secondary. While accepting that moral education is widely thought of as cross-curricular in nature, the argument is made that special programmes are required and that religious education teachers are best placed to provide them.

MORAL EDUCATION

In the early eighties Peter McPhail of the Schools Council Moral Education Project analysed the results of a survey conducted among boys and girls from English and Welsh schools. The young people were asked to describe examples of good and bad treatment they had received, and situations in which they were unsure about what to do. They were also asked about what they most looked forward to, what they feared most, the good and bad things about living then and what if anything they would like to see done about them.

The findings indicated that there had been significant changes in responses since similar surveys conducted by the Schools Council in the sixties and eary seventies. There appeared to be less emphasis among adolescents on the importance of making decisions for oneself, and there were signs of a growing fatalism especially in the 14-16 age group. As boys and girls grew older there was an increase in concern about the extent of violence in society, nuclear policy and the inadequacy of political leadership. There were also signs that the media had become much more influential in moulding attitudes and behaviour. McPhail concluded:

> "Our schools clearly ought to devote more time to the development of judgement about contemporary issues and to helping individuals become as morally independent as possible."[1]

In this section I want to explore some of the means by which this might be achieved by discussing two major strands which I discern within the wealth of literature relating to moral education. These concern first, the consideration of principles and their application and second, the development of abilities and attitudes.

A moral principle can be described as a rule for living which is considered to be universal. It is a rule which we want all people to adopt in all situations. Principles, however, may, and frequently do come into conflict. It is precisely this that makes the process of moral decision-making such a complex business. Should we always tell the truth even if it means hurting someone we love? How do I draw the line between protecting my children and allowing them the freedom to become independent? Should I remain loyal to my friend even if I disagree with what he has done?

Some might want to argue that different societies and cultures now, and in the past, exhibit different moral rules and principles. That moral codes are relative to particular societies and change as society changes. It is important to distinguish, however, between ethical 'ideals' and the concrete ways in which these have been applied at particular times and places. Principles such as justice or the concern for others cannot be defined or limited to a certain range of meanings. Over the centuries in fact their sphere of application has broadened to include all age groups, genders and peoples. Western society in the eighteenth and nineteenth centuries tolerated slavery, and within many archaic religions human sacrifice to placate the gods was the rule rather than the exception. Even today the principles of justice and concern for others are inadequately grasped resulting in homelessness, poverty, and oppression. John Hick has drawn our attention to the basic principle that it is evil to cause suffering to others and good to benefit others by easing or preventing their suffering. It is this principle, he says that is elaborated in the moral precepts of the great religious traditions. It starts from assumptions of fair dealing and respect for others' lives and property, and progresses towards its expression through generosity, forgiveness, kindness, love and compassion.[2]

Principles and their application

For R.S. Peters a principle is "that which makes a consideration relevant".[3] Suppose a person is wondering whether gambling is wrong and in thinking this through he takes into account the likely misery which would be caused to his or her family and friends. This shows he accepts the principle of considering other people's interests. It does not matter if he has trouble formulating the principle, says Peters, as long as he is able to show sensitivity to these considerations rather than to other less important ones. For Peters the practice of morality is about having reasons for actions. If we are convinced about the need to give reasons for our actions then this very conviction lays down a number of fundamental principles without which the whole search for reasons becomes unintelligible. These principles are not just optional or matters of choice for the person who thinks it important to give reasons for their actions. All moral, rational people therefore must accept such principles as fairness, truth-telling, freedom, consideration of interests, and respect for persons. When giving reasons for our actions we must insist on being fair to all parties. This means at the very least avoiding arbitrariness and ensuring that our reasons are based on relevant distinctions. In addition our reasons ought to be appropriate to the field of moral discourse, and be based on a careful consideration of interests and respect for persons. Finally we need to proceed on the basis that we always tell the truth otherwise the whole process of giving reasons for our actions becomes meaningless.[4]

For Peters then morality is based on a set of rationally deduced and justifiable principles. Moral education therefore must be a matter of getting children to adopt these principles and apply them in real situations. Clearly the learning and application of principles is not something within the reach of all children regardless of age. The facts of child development mean that the process of learning to reason from universal principles will be a long and gradual one. How then can children be encouraged to develop towards this? Peters calls this the 'paradox of moral education'. To resolve it Peters believes that 'habit formation' must play an important part in the moral development of young children. Children must be taught a set of basic rules as they grow up. Peters writes, "they can and must enter the palace of Reason through the courtyard of Habit and Tradition."[5]

The learning of rules, however, is not sufficient by itself. Children need to be taught as early as possible the reasons for rules and that far from being proven facts imposed by adults to keep them in line, rules are open to challenge, discussion and even revision. The aim of moral education is not to ensure children obey rules but to encourage them to seek justification for them and to subject them to criticism. Recognising the importance of the interests of others, for example, will be a gradual process of witnessing its expression in individuals through acts of unselfishness, generosity and forgiveness. The principle of freedom will be developed as young people come to terms with the dilemma of 'doing their own thing' while at the same time accepting that at some point constraints will be necessary to protect the interests of others. Principles will be developed through seeing them applied in a wide variety of situations of increasing complexity, where solutions are hard to obtain and judgements painful.

The process of moral reasoning has been the subject of lengthy study and investigation by Lawrence Kohlberg. He and his colleagues have investigated the structure of young people's thinking about moral issues by probing the reasons they gave in answer to certain moral dilemmas. Their research has led them to the conclusion that people think about moral issues at three different levels with two stages at each level. Kohlberg is concerned here with the changes in the quality of the way people think about moral matters. Each stage therefore has its own characteristics irrespective of content. The three levels are Preconventional, Conventional and Post-Conventional or Principled.

One way of thinking about the three levels is to think of them in terms of three different relationships between the self and society's rules and expectations. At Level 1 rules and social expectations are something external to the person. Doing what is right means not breaking the rules and acting to meet one's own interests. Young children are often heard to say 'that's not fair' when things don't go their way. Rules are obeyed primarily in order to avoid punishment. At Level 2 the person has identified him or her self with the rules and expectations of society, especially those of authority. Doing what is right means living up to what is expected by people close to you or what people generally expect from a daughter, brother, friend. Being 'good' is important through showing concern for others and exhibiting qualities such as trust and loyalty. Right also means contributing to society, the group or the institution. At Level 3 the person has differentiated him or her self from the rules and expectations of others and defines his values in terms of self-chosen principles. Doing what is right means making judgements based on such principles. Among the principles concerned are universal principles of justice, the equality of human rights and respect for the dignity of human beings.

A principled approach to morality therefore views moral conflict from the perspective of any human being, not just from the perspective of one's own society. When laws or rules within one's own group or society appear to violate the principle one acts in accordance with the principle. From the point of view of one's own society it might make sense to remain loyal to it even if this means taking up arms in its defence. This may conflict however with the principle of respect for life, leading a person to become a conscientious objector.[6] In Kohlberg's view teaching must be directed towards creating a degree of dissatisfaction in the student about his present state of knowledge of what it means to do what is right. This is to be done by exposing students to moral conflict situations for which he has no ready solution, and encouraging disagreement and argument about these situations with his peers.

Abilities and attitudes

The concentration on moral reasoning with its emphasis on principles and their application is likely to give the impression that morality is more concerned with rationality than with emotion, with logic rather than imagination. This would clearly be mistaken. Moral issues, whether of a personal or social nature, are things people care about and feel committed to doing something about. Morality is not just about reasoning, it is also about feelings and behaviour. It is important therefore that children do not see morality as a purely intellectual exercise. Kohlberg is frequently criticised for over-intellectualising the business of moral education, for concentrating on the development of moral thinking to the detriment of more affective aspects of the process. The affective aspects of morals cover positive motivations such as empathy and an attitude of concern for others, but it also includes more negative ones such as shame and guilt.

We should not attempt, however, any rigid separation of reason from feelings, the cognitive from the affective. Education is concerned with improving our understanding of the world and ourselves, both of which have a cognitive and an affective dimension. A person's display of emotion may be more or less rational although it is with its rationality that education is essentially concerned. A student may feel guilt at having taken home money found in the school corridor instead of handing it in. The task of moral education would be to explore such feelings. Is he or she acting on the basis of some notion of 'finders keepers'? If so can this be regarded as adequate? What are the principles involved here? What is the right thing to do in this situation? John Wilson writes:

"Being rational or reasonable, however, does not mean disregarding one's feelings, but trying to assess, guide or direct them in some coherent way."[7]

Wilson believes we need to help young people of all ages to understand their own and other people's emotions. By getting them to act out their emotions through role-play, games and simulated situations, they can be helped to understand themselves better. To become more emotionally educated is in an important sense intellectual. The aim is to provide young people with a better cognitive grasp of their own and other people's feelings rather than simply encourage self-expression for its own sake. It is not sufficient to realise how we feel, we need to understand why.[8] To be morally educated, argues Wilson, is to develop certain abilities and attitudes:

- The attitude that the needs, feelings and interests of others are equally as important as one's own.
- Awareness of one's own and other people's feelings and interests.
- Sufficient knowledge to be able to make informed decisions on moral issues.
- Ability to take account of the above in particular situations, so as to decide and act in accordance with them.[9]

The advantage of Wilson's suggestions is that they seem eminently suitable for all students regardless of age. Learning about ourselves and other people, about the rules which govern our relationships, about why people behave in certain ways is well within the reach of even the youngest school children. The use of literature or a short film sequence depicting a piece of social behaviour can, allied to discussion, be a useful means of promoting education in morality. By stopping at relevant points, asking questions, encouraging students to comment, teachers can help students to identify what they feel about various situations and why. Students might then be asked to act out and write about some of the situations they have been discussing, while all the time being encouraged to generalise from the particular situation being discussed, and to make predictions about themselves and others - what do you think is going to happen next? What would you do if you were in this situation? How would you feel? Do you think everyone would feel that way? For Wilson the stress is on developing the attitudes as well as the abilities necessary for deciding and acting morally. There is little reference to the content of morality in terms of specific principles such as we find in Peters.

Similarly Peter McPhail of the Schools Council Moral Education Project is as much concerned with cultivating attitudes and shaping behaviour as he is with developing problem-solving abilities. According to McPhail we learn moral values by observing the ways in which important people in our lives treat us and others. Morality is something we pick up by being around considerate people. McPhail makes consideration for the needs, feelings and interests of others the basis of his programme. Young people are to be helped to develop a 'considerate style of life'. As in Wilson there is not much emphasis on the content of morality. It is not the role of moral education, says McPhail, to persuade young people to accept the values we accept. Rather we should be helping them to work out their own values. The methodology of the Project is one of opening up choices, considering possible consequences, and leaving students to make up their own minds about what they would do in particular situations.

The Project material, called 'Lifeline', comprises three parts, 'In other people's shoes', 'Proving the rule', and 'What would you have done?' The first, **'In other people's shoes'** consists of situations built around common interpersonal problems experienced in the home, school or neighbourhood and contains three sections, 'Sensitivity', 'Consequences' and 'Points of View'. In 'Sensitivity' each situation is introduced by a picture and followed by the question, 'What do you do?' For example:
- You know that your best friend is doing something which is causing him or her to suffer. What do you do?
- You lend a coat to your cousin; when the coat is returned, there is a cigarette burn on the lapel. What do you do?
- An acquaintance of yours often butts in and tries to change the subject when you are talking to someone. What do you do?

'Consequences' is designed to help students think beyond one-to-one relationships and to take a third party into account. The basic question posed here is, what is likely to happen next? 'Points of View' tries to help students take the role of the other before saying what they would do in particular situations. Situations are arranged under sex attitudes, age, racial, religious and political conflict.

The second part, **'Proving the rule'** deals with instances of conflicts in personal relations as well as more complex conflicts of group interests and the issue of authority. The material does not emphasise current moral and social problems because "solutions to these problems are implicit in the approach."[10] It explores instead the problems that Paul, a young adolescent, encounters in various social settings - at school, in the home and at work. It deals with rules, principles and laws and what happens when these conflict. For example: Paul was helping with the school fund drive. It was Wednesday and he had promised to take Liz to the movies. But he was broke. He was 'borrowing' a few pounds from the fund when he was caught red-handed and sent to the Headmaster. The Headmaster called Paul's parents to tell them about the situation and to notify them that he was suspending Paul from school for a week.

1   Do you think that the Headmaster behaved fairly or unfairly in this situation? What would you have done if you were the Head?
2   How do you think Paul's parents would react to the situation? Do you think they might have punished him too? If so, how?
3   Think of some of the rules which people you know have broken and say
    (a) if you think the punishment they got was fair.
    (b) if not, what do you think a fair punishment might have been?

The third part, **'What would you have done?'** tries to widen students' moral perspective by looking at a number of social issues based on actual events in history, such as South Africa in 1904 dealing with the topic of compassion, and Amsterdam in 1944 dealing with persecution.

PERSONAL AND SOCIAL EDUCATION

In a recent discussion among a group of teachers about the relationships between religious, moral and social education, a question arose as to what was meant by social education. Although some of the teachers present actually taught social education the answer quickly came back, "Whatever you want it to mean." Interestingly, at no point during that discussion was any question raised about the meaning of religious or moral education. The uncertainty about the nature of social education seems to relate as much to content as it does to aims. A typical view of the content of a social education course is that it will include topics such as alcohol, smoking, sex, health and personal hygiene, safety, parenthood and the world of work. Or as one teacher is reputed to have said to a researcher, 'Social education is about drink, drugs and sex - all the things you're not supposed to do but enjoy doing most.' Content might also include, however, knowledge of ourselves, our environment, and society at large including an understanding of political and economic affairs.

Social education or social training?

In a survey of relevant literature Richard Pring picked out a number of different aims which have been attached to social education - to learn about the local society, to understand how society works, to learn to be responsible, to have the right social attitudes. Pring is critical of these as aims for social education chiefly on the basis that they fail as 'education'. For education would seem to imply at least some opportunity to develop the capacity to look critically at beliefs and values and to weigh evidence. The above aims betray a narrowness of vision which makes it difficult to acquire the standards of comparison necessary for a critical appreciation. They are concerned not just with understanding but with the inculcation of certain attitudes and ways of behaving. There is more to schooling, says Pring, than the socialisation of the young into the norms and values of society. Education is more than mere social training.[11] Similar criticisms I believe can be directed at 'Meeting Points', a document published several years ago by the Consultative Committee on the Curriculum in Scotland and aimed at the primary school. Here the long term aim of social education is "to establish understanding of the way in which our society works, and prepare them to participate fully, effectively and with confidence as responsible adults in that society."[12] To be socially effective, the document continues, means among other things:

- understanding the function or purpose of the group and the reasons for its formation.
- accepting the responsibilities which membership of the group implies and participating actively in the group's undertakings.
- understanding and appreciating the values held by the group and showing willingness to modify his own attitudes, behavior, interests and wishes accordingly.[13]

Social education as 'process'

In contrast J. Berridge has suggested that social education is better thought of as an 'enabling process' to help young people to acquire and develop skills; skills which will enable them to make the best of post-school opportunities, form happy and fulfilled relationships, to develop their talents to the full and to enjoy life. The purpose of such a social education programme is to develop in students those skills which will enable them to take control of their lives. Courses should be skill-based rather than knowledge-based without denying the importance of acquiring information and understanding concepts. Far from attempting to alter the attitudes and behaviour of students in line with society, social education ought to be providing the skills by which students can change society. He explains:

"Social education is an enabling process through which young people may acquire skills which will allow them to achieve a greater understanding of

society and to effect change within it."[14]
Berridge links this with the importance of using appropriate methodology in
the development of skills, providing students with opportunities to
participate in joint ventures both within and outwith the school as well as
working together in small groups.

This view of social education as a process of developing key skills and
attitudes is also seen as operating throughout the curriculum in all subjects.
The authors of a recent report on social education explain:

> "...the concept of social education central to this report leaves no doubt
> that this aspect of pupils' education has a great deal to do with the nature
> of the pupils' day-to-day learning experiences. The main concern should
> be to place in the forefront of attention the social orientation of the
> educational experience as a whole and in its parts. This social orientation
> can be defined as the extent to which the pupil is required to interact with
> others, ...to form attitudes in relation to others, ...and to develop a feeling
> of responsibility towards others."[15]

In his excellent little book, *Personal and Social Education*, John McBeath
gives an example of how such a 'social orientation' might be achieved using a
structured group discussion format in which students are expected to listen,
argue, make decisions and generally take responsibility for their own
learning. The situation is akin to Kohlberg's moral dilemmas or McPhail's
problem areas, except that it involves seven characters, each of whom might
be judged as being partly responsible for the death of one of their number.
Having told the story the teacher asks each student to take five minutes in
which to list the characters in terms of who was most responsible. When
they have done this they are put into groups of four or five and given twenty
minutes to reach an agreed order. In the discussion they are asked to observe
several ground rules; listen to other people's point of view, make sure
everyone gets a fair hearing, try to work out which are the strongest
arguments when supporting your decisions. At the end of the twenty
minutes the teacher asks one of the groups to justify their decision for putting
a particular character first in their order of priority. Other members of the
class are then encouraged to join in.[16]

McBeath is anxious to avoid the type of social education we saw at the
beginning of this section, which is often regarded as soft-centered, lacking a
critical dimension, and more to do with training than with education. Hence
he refers to the importance of students being open to criticism, challenging
the unacceptable, and being prepared to act against social injustice. Such
skills of challenge and confrontation, he points out, are generally played
down in schools but are the key to better institutional management as well as
personal effectiveness. The objectives of social education, he argues, can be

achieved within a variety of contexts, literature, history or religious education. Personal and social education therefore must be seen as a cross-curricular pursuit as well as a specific timetabled programme. He suggests that personal and social education should be directed at the following objectives:

- **coming to terms with yourself** - including the ability to distinguish your own opinions and beliefs from those of others; a willingness to examine your own situation and your own experience; an openness to others' perceptions of yourself, to criticism and to praise.
- **coming to terms with others** - including a respect for the rights of others; a sense of responsibility for, and accountability to, others; sensitivity to the feelings and position of others; the ability to challenge and confront views and behaviour that are unacceptable.
- **coming to terms with society** - including an understanding of the possibilities and constraints of individual action and choice; concern for individuals and groups who are discriminated against in our society; a knowledge of strategies and resources for responding to injustice and discrimination; a respect for legitimate authority.[17]

Similarly, Kenneth David, writing for a Schools Council working party describes the content of personal and social education as including "the teaching and informal activities which are planned to enhance the development of knowledge, understanding, attitudes and behaviours, concerned with:

> oneself and others;
> social institutions, structures and organisations;
> and social and moral issues."[18]

In order to find out the issues which concern people David suggests that schools might discuss with students the planning of social education courses. This may serve to identify topics to do with say relationships and careers which research has indicated are the source of a good deal of worry among young people. It will also help to promote a key objective, that of "acquiring confidence in, and an ability to express, their own reasoned opinions."[19]

Social education or moral education?

All the descriptions of personal and social education we have looked at disclose an intimate connection with moral education. Richard Pring writes:

> "Values permeate the whole of personal and social education, and moral development is at the centre."[20]

From this it would seem that much of what might be done in social education will also meet the objectives for moral education and vice versa. This will be particularly true of primary where specific concerns relating to puberty, adulthood and employment have not yet surfaced. This of course does not imply that younger children are not interested in finding out about themselves, and the world around them. It is simply to say that their social horizons are more limited and their powers of judgement at an earlier stage of development. On the contrary, as well as being involved in aspects of health and sex education children can enjoy learning more about their own feelings and the feelings of others through a whole range of activities. Through identifying with the characters in stories such as *The Lion, the Witch, and the Wardrobe,* or *The story of Rama and Sita,* children can see the qualities of friendship, loyalty, and courage in action and take part, albeit from a safe place, in the enduring struggle between good and evil. In stories such as *Badger's Parting Gifts,* and *The Owl who was Afraid of the Dark,* children can share the sadness at losing a friend, and the fear of being unable to cope with the unknown. By writing, drawing and talking with each other and the teacher, they can move with the narrative until the sadness changes to joy and the fear is unmasked. By taking part in role play and exercising helpfulness and generosity through action in the community, children can be encouraged to see things from a different perspective. Through these and other activities children will be helped to understand their own feelings, and to develop a genuine concern for others and an active desire to promote their welfare.

In the secondary sector where students are much closer to adulthood and the world of work, there is a greater need for special courses in careers, health, parenthood and relationships generally, as well as opportunities to consider moral and social issues. The relationship between moral and social issues is a fluid one and not always clear. Many moral issues will also be social issues but all social issues do not necessarily have a moral dimension. Many subjects will want to cover important social issues which are not resolved primarily by reference to moral values, although they may harbour moral assumptions. For example - Can sanctions bring about the collapse of apartheid in South Africa? In the light of recent changes in Eastern Europe does the Soviet Union still pose a threat to the West? To what extent is racism a problem in our society? How should we respond to the dangers of increased alcoholism among young people?

Religious education will be concerned with "personal and social issues emanating from religious and moral values".[21] In other words it will be concerned with those issues which cannot be resolved without reference to religious and/or moral values. For example - How important are the rights of the mother in the debate about abortion? Can the taking of life in war ever be justified? How far ought we to pursue equality between the sexes? What limits, if any, should we place on embryo experimentation? Some social issues, however, need to take account of specific religious values or perhaps more accurately, of the particular priorities assigned within a religious tradition to general moral values and principles. For example - What should be done when the values of a religious minority clash with those of society? Should the Churches speak out against Government policies? Do separate religious schools increase religious and social divisions? A certain amount of overlap is probably inevitable and perhaps desirable here between subjects like RE, PSE, English, history, modern studies. A properly conducted curriculum audit, however, could ensure that students are being exposed to a wide range of moral and social issues within local, national and world spheres.

In their survey of personal and social education courses HMI found that the overriding concern of such courses was to help prepare students for adult life. They were concerned to help students develop self-awareness, and to understand the nature of personal and social relationships as well as aspects of the social, economic and political world in which they live. The most frequently featured themes related to health education, careers, political education and world issues, moral and religious education, and personal relationships and responsibilities. As far as religious education was concerned 50% of schools included it as part of their personal and social education courses.[22]

Grimmitt has recently claimed that this development has had a number of results "most of which are unfavourable to religious education."[23] It is not uncommon, he says, to find teachers and the media expressing the view that religious education has been replaced by PSME. This is in fact the case in many schools, Grimmitt argues, where religious education has been replaced with courses "which provide no opportunities for the exploration of religious issues or even of matters to which an understanding of religion has any relevance."[24] Although in Scotland only a few schools seem to have integrated religious education into a social education programme the results appear to support Grimmitt's conclusions. HMI reports that "religious education suffered badly in the new arrangements". Where there was no experienced specialist teacher to advise on the construction of courses the religious education element was often "uninformed and contrived... Frequently the time allocated to the whole social education programme failed to take account of the extended nature of the course and teachers were unable to do justice to the agreed objectives."[25]

On the other hand some have argued strongly in favour of integration in the form of a Faculty of Personal and Social Education. This would serve to raise the status of this area of the curriculum while at the same time provide a career structure for teachers eager to teach RE, ME, Careers and Health education. One of the difficulties with integration in this area is that it involves taking together distinct forms of knowledge with their own key concepts and criteria for truth. A faculty of personal and social education could be looking to religion, philosophy, psychology, sociology and politics in the preparation of courses. Fewer problems are likely to be encountered if the issues arising from these disciplines are avoided or tackled only superficially. The HMI survey on personal and social education found precisely this:

> "...there was a tendency for teachers to treat only superficially potentially controversial aspects of courses" and the emphasis placed on the transmission of knowledge meant that opportunities for analysis and judgement were severely limited.[26]

Moral and social issues, however, do frequently involve knowledge from a range of disciplines. Issues relating to the implications of living in a plural society for example will involve political, economic, sociological, and religious factors. In order to deal adequately with such issues this knowledge must be acquired somehow and an appropriate context needs to be found to bring it together. This context though need not be an elaborate one in the form of a faculty of personal and social education. Hirst writes:

> "Subjects, suitably constructed, can do that, though they have only rarely done it satisfactorily. What we need are units... which do not seek to 'integrate' the forms of knowledge, or cut across them for no real reason, but which are true to the dependence of some elements of knowledge on knowledge of other kinds."[27]

In the next section I want to pursue this point by arguing for more attention to be paid to courses in moral education particularly within religious education.

A SPECIAL ROLE FOR RE?

Recently I attended a conference on moral education involving teachers from a wide variety of subjects areas, parents and college lecturers. One speaker received considerable support for the view that there was something distinctly disagreeable about RE teachers being involved in moral education, particularly without the appropriate knowledge and training. The training of religious education teachers, he said, does not equip them sufficiently for an additional role as moral educators. This was not a matter for regret, however, since moral education should in any case be kept separate from religious education. Moral values must not be thought to be dependent on having a religious belief. I will not enter the debate here as to whether moral values are or are not independent of religion. Suffice to say that it is not a simple matter of disagreement between those who consider themselves religious and those who do not. Many Christians observe that people are capable of moral insight without having made a religious confession of faith. They conclude that moral values are rooted in the very structure of our human nature, and it is that nature which is rooted in our relationship to God. Those values therefore can be recognised and shared by all who share that human nature.

How we keep ME separate from religious education within the curriculum, who would be responsible for it and whether it is indeed desirable to do so are all questions that admit of no easy answers.

In Scotland there has emerged a consensus on the adoption of religion and morality as one single mode or area of experience within the curriculum. The Munn report in 1977 originally postulated eight modes with religion and morality as two separate modes. In 1982 the Scottish Education Department approved the conflation of these two modes into one single mode, 'Religious and Moral Studies'.[28] This position has been consistently maintained although not without a few hiccups along the way. In a number of official documents for example, religious and moral education are seen as "important aspects of social education".[29] And in one letter from the Scottish Education Department a brand new mode appeared, the 'Religious, Moral and Social Education Mode', although this was later admitted to have been a mistake.[30] In the latest document the 'Religious and Moral Education' mode is said to reflect "two distinct but interlinked areas of activity".[31] Distinct because as the speaker I referred to above implied, one can happily engage in the process of moral reasoning and action without courting allegiance to any religious belief system. One can in practice engage in moral education without reference to religion. Interlinked because morality is a dimension within all religions. The study of religion must involve the study of morality as part of religion. There can be no religious education without moral education. If both positions are to be taken seriously we need to ensure that religious education is not seen to be taking on the sole responsibility for moral education in the school situation, by encouraging other curriculum areas to examine their contribution. Nevertheless the implication here is clear; that religious education staff have a special role to play in the provision of moral education.

None of what has been said so far, however, implies special programmes in moral education. Moral education might still be delivered through the concerted contribution of a variety of subject disciplines. Whether in fact subject teachers will be eager to become more involved in aspects of moral education is doubtful. In a survey of Scottish schools 78% of headteachers and only 65% of teachers endorsed morality as an area of study for all students.[32] The contribution of religious education will be to offer a range of views concerning how other people live and understand the world. With older students the relationships between what we think human beings are and the way we ought to treat them could be explored. In the process of making moral decisions we cannot escape the influence of our beliefs and assumptions regarding the nature of humankind. These beliefs and assumptions need to be discussed and examined carefully with young people, starting lower down the school perhaps with a discussion of the similarities and differences between human beings and the rest of the animal kingdom. As long as moral education through subject disciplines or personal and social education is seen to be done and not simply assumed then this is at least a step in the right direction of its effective delivery.

The case for special programmes

A good case can be made, however, for including specially devised courses for moral education. The basis of such a case has already been argued in Scotland with respect to social education. In Scotland most schools have policy frameworks relating to personal development and social education. Such policies generally see personal and social education as a cross-curricular activity and allude to the responsibility of all teachers for this. We noted in the last section how this might be done through students' day-to day learning experiences. In addition, special programmes of social education in areas such as careers, relationships, parenthood and health have usually been developed in order to avoid gaps in essential knowledge and to ensure a more progressive and coherent set of learning experiences for students.

Similarly then with moral education. Conducting moral education solely within curricular subjects may result in important aspects being omitted. For example if we follow through the thinking of R.S.Peters, can we guarantee that his central principles will form the basis of work in moral education? And what about the skills of moral reasoning which John Wilson has highlighted for us? How can we ensure that appropriate opportunities are provided for students to develop these? With the best will in the world the development of these principles and skills is likely to be a random affair if it is left to curricular subjects alone. Opportunities for exploring issues will arise frequently within the study of literature or history or social studies. Whether these are pursued consistently and with effect will depend on the existence of a well thought out school policy which indicates the kind of content and skills appropriate for different age groups having taken account perhaps of Kohlberg's work on the development of moral reasoning. Subject departments would need to examine their existing courses in order to relate aspects of the school's policy on moral education to particular topics or themes. Even if this were accomplished there would still be a problem of finding sufficient time especially in the later years of schooling with external examinations adding to the ever present pressures to cover content. Moreover, as we have already noted, the study of moral issues demands an acquaintance with the facts, scientific, economic and political. Many of the moral problems in contemporary society are difficult precisely because the facts are complex. Students must learn that before we can make decisions on issues such as abortion, human embryo research, or the just war, it is important to know the facts. Can we expect teachers of english or science to provide the necessary time required of such an exercise? Or is it more likely that discussion of,say, euthanasia will amount to little more than a 'frank' exchange of views. This may well be valuable in its own way but it is not sufficient if we are interested in providing students with the skills to recognise and deal adequately with complex moral issues.

We have already mentioned briefly the close links between religion and morality. Beliefs about humankind and the world and the relationship of these to the transcendent always result in rules governing how people should behave. Moral controversy is inherent in much of human activity and issues of morality are raised within the ethical traditions of all the major religions of the world. Whether Christian, Buddhist or agnostic we all struggle with problems of freedom and authority, justice and injustice, right and wrong. In addition to a code for living religions add distinctive and positive ideals to a person's way of life influencing how he or she spends their time and money and the kind of relationships they form. Religious teaching, by giving weight to particular principles, can affect a person's priorities and decisions. For Muslims personal freedom is subordinate to the role of authority, and Islamic teaching sets limits on all aspects of their personal and social life. For Hindus belief in the doctrine of 'ahimsa' can engender a reverence for all forms of life not seen among people generally. And in Christianity emphasis on the social implications of Jesus'teaching has created a concern among Christians for the poor and the oppressed at various times throughout its history, not least of all the present day. Also religions have much to say about the significance of morality. The religious person sees the moral life as part of an overall purpose which is wider and deeper than the moral. In other words for religions right behaviour and relationships are constitutive of salvation.

Some recent work done by Kohlberg and Power confirms the close relationship between religion and morality. They too argue that religion and morality are discrete aspects of experience but there are also ways in which they relate. Moral reasoning is the way in which a person decides between conflicting interests, and decisions are based on a developing sense of fundamental principles. Moral judgements are concerned with the reasons one brings to bear on particular issues. Religious judgement is concerned with questions that go beyond immediate problems to ultimate questions such as, what is the purpose of my existence? and why be good? It is concerned with the search for an all-embracing explanation to explain moral and all other activity. By using Kohlberg's moral dilemmas together with questions from James Fowler's work on faith development they compared progress in religious thinking with progress in moral reasoning. They found that there was eighty one per cent overall agreement between the Stages used for religious thinking by Fowler and those for moral reasoning by Kohlberg. In Stages 1-3 there was one hundred per cent agreement, the divergence occurring at the later stages, where moral reasoning tended to be one stage higher than religious reasoning. They concluded that "moral judgement is a necessary but not sufficient condition for religious reasoning at least at the higher stages."[33]

The special relationship between religion and morality requires a special role for teachers of religious education in promoting moral education. It must fall to religious education to help provide a planned and systematic approach to this area of the curriculum, so that students can develop the ability to identify, examine, and make judgements on a wide range of moral issues. I am not confident, however, that we are in a position to do this successfully at present. Much work still needs to be done before moral education can be seen to be an integral part of students' personal and social development. Not least, the time allocated for religious education in most schools must be extended if teachers are to take on an increased responsibility for moral education. Only in schools which can show that their personal and social development courses contribute significantly to students' moral development will this not be necessary. In Scotland it is significant that a study of moral issues now forms a compulsory part of both Standard Grade and Higher Religious Studies courses. There are ethics courses included as part of a range of national certificate modules and moral issues feature among a number of short courses in religious studies recently approved by the Scottish Examination Board for the 14-16 age group. Below I have tried to set out a framework of objectives which teachers might use for the study of personal and social issues within religious education.

Knowing the Facts
Before reaching moral decisions it is important to understand the issue being studied as fully as possible. This will usually mean coming to grips with the body of information relating to the issue, whether it be economic, political, social or religious. Particular moral decisions rest ultimately on assumptions and beliefs about the nature of ourselves as human beings, and the nature of the world in which we live.
- knowledge and understanding of how others live and view the world.
- knowledge and understanding of beliefs relating to the nature of human life.
- knowledge and understanding of moral values and principles within selected religious traditions.
- knowledge and understanding of relevant information e.g. economic; political; social.

Making up Your Mind
The second category reflects the need for some degree of independent judgement and free choice to be exercised in the making of moral decisions.

It assumes that 'having principles' is closely connected with being moral and that there are certain principles which are fundamental to the whole process of making moral judgements.
e.g. consideration for others; fairness / justice; freedom; telling the truth.
- ability to think in general or universal terms.
- ability to demonstrate appreciation of different viewpoints on an issue.
- ability to apply general moral values and principles to a particular issue.
- ability to express and justify an opinion on a range of moral issues.

Becoming Mature
Moral issues are things people care about and feel committed to doing something about. Students must realise that they are not just concerned with intellectual argument here. We need to focus also on feelings.
- ability to understand ones own feelings and the feelings of others.
- ability to imagine oneself in the position of others.
- development of concern for others and desire to promote their welfare.

NOTES AND BIBLIOGRAPHY

1 Peter McPhail·'The Morality of Communication' in *The Ethical Dimension of the School Curriculum,* ed. Lionel Ward, University of Swansea, 1982, p108.
2 John Hick *An Interpretation of Religion* MacMillan, 1989, p314.
3 R.S.Peters 'Concrete Principles and the Rational Passions' in *Moral Development and Moral Education* Unwin, 1981, p66
4 ibid. p70-73
5 R.S.Peters 'Reason and Habit: The Paradox of Moral Education' op cit p51
6 Lawrence Kohlberg 'Moral Stages and Moralisation: The Cognitive-Developmental Approach' in *Moral Development and Behaviour* ed. Thomas Lickona, Holt Rinehart and Winston, 1976, p33-35.
7 John Wilson *A Teachers Guide to Moral Education* Geoffrey Chapman, 1973, p31.
8 John Wilson *Education in Religion and the Emotions* Heinemann, 1971, p162ff
9 Wilson, op cit 1973, p28.
10 Peter McPhail *Moral Education in the Secondary School* Longman, 1972, p112.
11 Richard Pring 'Socialisation as an aim of Education', in *Social Education and Social Understanding* ed. Pring and Elliot, University of London, 1975 ,p17-21
12 Meeting Points, Committee on Primary Education, Scottish Curriculum   Development Service, 1985, para.2.3
13 ibid para 2.4
14 J.Berridge 'The Social Education Process, in Religious and Moral Education' in *Secondary Schools* ed. Howard Marratt, R.E.Council of England and Wales, 1985, p32.
15 Social Education in Scottish Schools, Consultative Committee on the Curriculum, 1984, para 3.20.
16 John MacBeath *Personal and Social Education* Scottish Academic Press, 1988, p57

17 ibid Chapter 6.
18 Kenneth David *Personal and Social Education in Secondary Schools*, Schools Council, Longman, 1983, p18.
19 ibid p21.
20 Richard Pring *Personal and Social Education in the Curriculum* Hodder and Stoughton, 1984, p6
2 Curriculum Design for the Secondary Stages, Scottish Consultative Council on the Curriculum, 1989, p30
22 A Survey of Personal and Social Education Courses in Some Secondary Schools, DES, 1988, p4
23 Michael Grimmitt *Religious Education and Human Development* McCrimmons, 1987, p261.
24 ibid p262
25 Learning and Teaching in Religious Education, Scottish Education Department, 1986, para 4.35.

26 op cit DES, 1988, p21.
27 Paul Hirst *Knowledge and the Curriculum* Routledge, 1974, p145.
28 The Munn and Dunning Reports, 'Framework for Decision', SED, 1982, para 4.11
29 See 'Primary Education in the Eighties' and 'Meeting Points' para 2.6.
30 A letter to the Scottish Association of Advisers in Religious Education from the Scottish Education Department, 14 April, 1988.
31 op cit SCCC, 1989, p30
32 'Achievement, Assessment and Reporting', Selected Essays by Bryan Dockrell, Scottish Council for Research in Education, 1988, p43.
33 Marion Smith 'Religious Education' in *Lawrence Kohlberg: Consensus and Controversy* ed Modgil and Modgil, Falmer Press, 1985, p281.

6 LEARNING TO EVALUATE

Begins by assessing the importance of R.J. Goldman before looking at the work of E.A. Peel in relation to adolescent judgement. The cognitive and affective aspects of evaluating are described with particular reference to primary schools, and recent suggestions concerning the teaching of philosophy and reasoning skills are examined. Some criteria for evaluating in the secondary school are set out together with examination questions designed to test them. Several examples of students' responses are also included.

THE STRUCTURE OF STUDENTS' THINKING

There are few commentators around today quite as witty and insightful as Adrian Mole. In his diary entry for Tuesday the tenth of May he writes:
"I keep getting anxiety attacks every time I think about the exams. I know I'm going to fail. My overriding problem is that I'm too intellectual. I am constantly thinking about things, like: was God married? and: if Hell is other people, is Heaven empty? These thoughts overload my brain, causing me to forget facts. Such as: the average rainfall in the average Equational Forest and other boring stuff."[1]

I think Mole has put his finger here on a widespread weakness within our school system. In so far as public examinations dominate education particularly in the middle to upper secondary, they have hitherto emphasised the learning of facts rather than their application. Mole seems convinced he is heading for certain failure since he is unable to remember facts, yet considers himself an intellectual because he is constantly "thinking" about things.

This apparent opposition between "facts" and "thought" has given rise within some subjects to a lively debate between a content approach to teaching and a skills approach. True, both in GCSE and in Standard Grade, examinations are moving towards less "facts" and more "thinking", but the relationship between them is by no means a straightforward one. Many would argue that thinking about anything requires a sound basis of knowledge and understanding; that the ability to think critically may be in fact more closely linked to specific knowledge and understanding than to the need for developing a certain set of skills. It was the late Lawrence Stenhouse who wrote:
"The most important characteristic of knowledge is that one can think with

it... it is a structure to sustain creative thought and provide frameworks for judgement".[2]

Or to turn this around; in order to think critically and make judgements a person must have a thorough understanding of the area in which he is being critical. This view has important implications for learning and teaching, not least for learning to evaluate. Although it is unlikely that students will learn how to evaluate without sufficient opportunities to practice the art, it implies that the skill will be less developed and less effective if knowledge has been presented in an inappropriate or unstructured way.

R.J. Goldman

It was not until the 1960s that empirical evidence began to appear suggesting that a change in the quality of thinking about religion occurred in children and adolescents. Foremost among the researchers was Ronald Goldman. Using interviews Goldman gathered information on the level of religious thinking of pupils in English schools. In his final sample two hundred school pupils were interviewed between the ages of six and seventeen years. Goldman asked questions about three pictures and three biblical stories. The pictures were a family entering church, a child praying alone and a child looking at a mutilated bible. From preliminary work these pictures revealed most clearly pupils' understanding of the concepts of church, prayer and bible. The three stories chosen from an original eight were Moses and the Burning Bush, the Crossing of the Red Sea and the Temptations of Jesus. As a result of his studies Goldman found that children's thinking about religion closely corresponded to Piaget's view that there is a continuum of thinking which follows a sequence of three stages.

> "We can therefore say with confidence" claimed Goldman, "that there is a sequence, a pattern through which children appear to pass, at varying speeds, which closely corresponds, in religious thinking, to an intuitive stage, a concrete operational stage and a formal and abstract operational stage".[3]

Goldman suggested, however, that the development of religious thinking was slower than the development of thinking in other subject areas. The transition between the intuitive and concrete stages was about 7-8 years, and the transition between concrete and abstract was about 13-14 years. Goldman's study of religious thinking has spawned a great deal of research and debate throughout the world, in the United States, Scandinavia, as well as in Britain. Much of this post-Goldman research has concentrated on the task of testing whether or not there are stages of religious thinking and at what ages they occur. Nicola Slee writes:

> "By and large the results appear to corroborate Goldman's account of the development of religious thinking."[4]

The work of Goldman, however, is often regarded as unnecessarily rationalistic, concentrating as it did on the intellect and the ability to reason. Critics argue that it lacks an appreciation of the symbolic and imaginative aspects of religious language. Goldman's emphasis on the cognitive, it is said, needs to be supplemented by other approaches, particularly in the primary. Goldman's findings drew attention to the fact that children in the concrete thinking stage misunderstand symbolic religious statements and take them literally. As a result we need to be careful when selecting biblical material for particular age-groups, since we may not be able to convey enough of the theological meaning to avoid misunderstanding.

As with literature generally, there are stories which are difficult or inappropriate for most children at a particular stage. Professional decisions have to be made about whether a story is or is not suitable for children in Primary one. But perhaps we should not be too concerned about ensuring that children always grasp the 'correct' theological interpretation, and be more concerned to allow a story to speak for itself at an intuitive and imaginative level. In practice, this means that some biblical stories, usually considered more appropriate in late primary might well be used at earlier stages. For example, the story of the Flood is usually recommended for children aged 9-11. In a recent syllabus the story of Noah can be found in a unit for children in Primary one, but not to teach how God dealt with the problem of evil by drowning the whole of mankind. Instead it is part of a series of lessons on the continuing changes in nature, with the intention of evoking feelings of interest and wonder. The story is told as a celebration of life and the rainbow, which God uses as a sign of his covenant with the world, is used as an image of hope. Although the rains may come, there is always the sun, and together they make the world beautiful.[5]

E.A. Peel

Although Peel directed Goldman's thesis at Birmingham University in the early 1960's, he himself did not make use of the Piagetian categories of intuitive, concrete and abstract thinking. Instead he employed the three related categories of 'restricted', 'circumstantial' and 'imaginative' judgements. Peel's work is not directed specifically at the development of religious thinking but at the general qualitative change which he believes occurs in thinking around adolescence. His studies show that Piaget's ages for reaching the stage where abstract problems can be tackled effectively, is rather optimistic. Like Goldman he suggests that 13-14 years is about right. Peel's work on adolescent thinking is extremely important for secondary school teachers for a number of reasons.

- First, whereas Goldman's work is most relevant to students' understanding of biblical stories and related concepts, Peel's work on adolescent judgement is applicable across a wide area of the Religious

Education curriculum.

- Second, like Piaget, Goldman concentrated his studies on children's ability to reason. Although he recognised that individuals have feelings and attitudes which determine to some extent the direction of their thinking, he nevertheless put this on one side. Peel, however, sees the mental powers of adolescents not only in terms of ability to reason at an abstract level, but also in terms of increased awareness, creativity and imagination.

- Third, although Peel's research does not represent a comprehensive account of cognitive development, his conclusions regarding students' ability to make judgements certainly represent one of the most important aspects of thinking. It is particularly appropriate given the recent shifts in emphasis within GCSE and Standard Grade from receiving and recalling information to involving pupils actively in discussion, enquiry and evaluation.

Peel studied the reasoning abilities of secondary school children by inviting them to make judgements over a wide range of problems and situations closely related to the tasks they are expected to perform in the classroom. He investigated the maturity of their judgement by examining the quality of their answers. According to Peel the central feature of the adolescent's intellectual life is the emerging ability to imagine possibilities. These possibilities may be conjured up in the form of ideas, theories, generalisations, cause-and-effect relations, and analogies. Imagining such possibilities implies thinking beyond the limited information associated with a given passage or body of content. By judgement Peel understands that form of thinking which is required whenever we are faced with a situation for which we have no ready-made answer. In addition he means those situations and problems for which there is no single correct answer but rather a range of answers none of which particularly stands out. Peel writes:

> "The transition from content-dominated to possibility-invoking answers seemed to be the pre-dominant feature of early and mid-adolescent thinking".[6]

The following example gives some impression of the nature of his researches. Students aged 11-15 were given the following passage and queston:

> "All large cities have art galleries and Italy is exceptionally rich in art treasures. Many people travel to Italy, especially to enjoy these old paintings, books and sculptures. Floods in the Florence area recently damaged many of these great works. Old paintings are rate, valuable and beautiful and should be kept safely stored.
>
> Q. Are the Italians to blame for the loss of the paintings and art treasures?"[7]

The answers to the questions were put into three categories. Each category represented an increased level of maturity of judgement.

1. Restricted (e.g. No; because they've got lots of treasures)
2. Circumstantial (e.g. I don't think they are. I think it was just the weather, and the rain had to come.)
3. Imaginative (e.g. Well, not completely, they could have been kept safe, unless the floods took them completely by surprise. I suppose they did, but it might be best to protect them in glass cages).

Only a small number of answers were received in category '1' which were characterised by irrelevant guesses, a lack of understanding as in the example above, or consisted merely of bits of the passage repeated verbatim. Although such answers were very much in a minority overall, Peel reminds us they need to be catered for in any teaching programme. The example in category '2' was typical of the responses from those children between 11 and 14. Few of the responses in category '3' were given by youngsters between 11 and 13 years old. Most were given by those in the 13 to 15 age range. The crucial transition for adolescents, that between circumstantial responses, logical but based on the information given, and imaginative responses, making use of other ideas and experiences, seems to emerge about 14 years.

The act of judgement then entails several elements:
- First, there is this ability to imagine possibilities, to invoke possible explanations or hypotheses. The number of possibilities which students come up with, however, cannot be taken as the sole measure of creativity. Some will be unacceptable if they are not realistically related to the question under discussion. In others the quality of the explanation which accompanies it will indicate greater maturity.
- Second, there is the ability to select the most appropriate explanation or hypothesis and reject the least desirable ones. At its most developed this will involve weighing up the merits of each possibility against the situation it purports to explain and developing and sustaining an argument.

Peel descibes a number of studies which show the difficulties encountered by adolescents when tackling problems involving the selection and elimination of hypotheses, even when those hypotheses are given to them along with all the supporting evidence. As teachers, it seems, we need to continually draw students' attention to alternative possibilities if we are to help them develop their ability to distinguish between competing explanations. And when preparing questions and marking schemes for tests and examinations we need to allow the results of such research to inform our experience, since as Peel observes:

"...not before the age of 15 can we expect to obtain systematic and coherent deductive argument".[8]

A variation on the second ability above is when pupils are asked not to imagine an explanation but rather to examine one. This involves pupils in expressing their opinions and justifying them in the light of available evidence. The following questions seem to be testing these abilities and are taken from a number of recent Ordinary Grade Religious Studies papers set by the Scottish Examination Board.

1. **Imagining possibilities**
   What difficulties would a Hindu find in following the principle of ahimsa?
   What difficulties might a person today have with the Resurrection?

2. **Selecting and rejecting alternative explanations**
   How far does the title "king" seem appropriate to Jesus with reference to his later life?
   How far is Zionism a religious rather than a political movement?
   How far can the custom of arranged marriages survive in a non-Muslim country?

3. **Examining a given point of view or hypothesis.**
   Some Christians believe that the festival of Christmas has become too commercialised. Do you agree? Give reasons for your answer.
   Do you think that Gandhi was realistic in expecting Hindus and Muslims to live together in peace in one country? Give reasons for your answer.
   Explain what "devout" means and say whether you agree that it is more difficult for a Muslim to be devout in a city. Give reasons for your answer

COGNITIVE AND AFFECTIVE

While we in Scotland were preparing our own report on Standard Grade Religious Studies we had before us the National Criteria on Religious Studies for England and Wales. I recall that we found particularly helpful the statement on evaluating, which talked in terms of "a thoughtful personal response". This pointed to the value of a critical approach to our subject which encompassed the affective as well as the cognitive. We have already noted the importance of imagination in Peel's analysis of what is involved in making judgements. I was convinced then, as I still am, that there is nothing to be gained from attempting to distinguish the cognitive and the affective within the process of evaluating. As I have already noted many of the statements under "self-understanding" in the Secondary Examination Council's report on Draft Criteria reflect our own understanding of the evaluative process. Greater self-understanding will be achieved hopefully, but the means to this end is very much dependent on developing the skills of evaluating, and applying these to our own beliefs and values as well as to those within the various religious traditions.

The distinction which we noted earlier between personal and impersonal evaluation also suggests both a cognitive and an affective dimension within the process of evaluation. Impersonal evaluation involves making judgements about the truth claims, beliefs and practices of different religious traditions, while personal evaluation contributes more directly to self-understanding by asking pupils to confront religions with questions which relate to their own experience of life so far. We noted too that this distinction is difficult to draw in practice. Although such questions are intended to contribute to self-understanding and therefore fall within the affective dimension, there is clearly a strong cognitive element here also. As John Greer has written, "religious insight and understanding cannot be analysed neatly into the cognitive and affective domains."[9]

It is all too easy to gain the impression that evaluation and critical thinking are purely cognitive processes. By emphasising the need to develop skills of reasoning, and by providing opportunities for students to 'examine' the arguments, we imply that the process can only be objective and academic. Yet, when I am asked to express and justify my opinion, I may also be revealing strong convictions sustained by long established attitudes. One of the fears sometimes expressed about students evaluating is that judgements and opinions are likely to be superficial and premature, based as they will be on a less than adequate understanding. This fear, it seems to me, emerges particularly in relation to fundamental Christian beliefs such as incarnation and resurrection. Can we really accept a situation, it is said, where students are rejecting the validity of such beliefs on the basis of their understanding at the age of fifteen? A number of things are relevant here. If students are to learn to evaluate they must get involved in the process of evaluating at every opportunity even at the risk of some superficiality. We cannot postpone such learning opportunities until some undetermined future date when the degree of understanding can be considered adequate. Granted, such judgements must be seen as tentative and provisional leaving open the possibility that students may change their position at a later date. The view of knowledge and understanding as being essentially open-ended is much more likely to be adopted by students if their opinions are seen to be of value and taken seriously, than if they are being asked merely to assimilate a Christian understanding without opportunity to 'say what they think'. We cannot in any case prevent students from 'thinking what they think'. Students will form opinions about resurrection or reincarnation or the existence of God. As teachers our task is to help make these judgements more informed. Moreover, Christian beliefs must be seen to be as open to critical evaluation as are the beliefs of other religions if we are to avoid any charge of bias or indoctrination.

To appreciate fully the affective aspect of evaluating it is necessary to see the process as one of engagement with a particular body of knowledge, whatever that may be. Divorce the skills from the context in which they are to be applied, and all too quickly they become ends in themselves rather than means to improving understanding and self-confidence. The movement for the teaching of reasoning or thinking-skills, which began in the U.S.A. and has been gathering momentum in this country, is open to just such a criticism.[10] Its supporters insist that there are, as well as specific skills of thinking in separate subject disciplines, general skills of thinking, which should be taught at appropriate levels even to primary children. According to W.D. Robinson, a number of other principles are shared to different degrees by all those working in this field. Among these are, the idea that the best way of developing such skills is through discussion methods, that the starting point for such discussion should be the pupils own interests and questions, and that the best way of tackling problems related to the transfer of such skills is through encouraging discussion of a large number of examples from a variety of subject areas.[11] These ideas, and the work, for example, of Professor Lipman in the U.S.A. have led some in this country to argue that there should be incorporated into the curriculum "a clear and definite strategy for developing reasoning skills in children".[12]

Not everyone, however, is convinced. One of the staunchest critics of the movement is John McPeck.[13] Robinson incorrectly ascribes to him the view that there are no such things as general thinking-skills. What McPeck actually says is that there is no such general skill as 'critical thinking', because critical thinking is always critical thinking about something. In other words the criteria for the application of general thinking skills vary from field to field. Within Standard Grade a number of subjects, notably the social subjects and religious studies have included 'evaluating' as an element to be assessed. Art and Design uses the term 'critical activity' and in religious studies we did consider at an early stage the term 'critical thinking'. On the face of it there is a great deal of similarity in the terms used suggesting that evaluating or critical thinking does have an identifiable meaning recognised across a range of subjects. When it comes to applying this to distinct areas some interesting differences begin to appear. In modern studies, for example, evaluating involves such skills as recognising lack of objectivity in sources. In history evaluating means, among other things, making judgements about actions and events in the past. And in religious studies it includes considering the implications of beliefs, practices and viewpoints. McPeck believes that critical thinking cannot be divorced from the knowledge and skills associated with a particular subject area. Critical thinking about an historical question, for example, will require the knowledge and skills of the historian, such as the ability to set a source in its historical context.

This view is reflected in the findings of much recent research. This indicates that through practice students can improve remarkably their ability to perform tasks of reasoning and problem solving. Such improvements, however, also depend heavily on students being presented with well organised structures of knowledge and seem to be specific to a relatively narrow area of expertise. There appears to be little transfer from one area to another. Skill in solving problems in physics does not transfer to history or economics. Although there are general skills, some related to the use of logic, these are rather weak in comparison to the more specific skills within given subject areas. In a recent survey of the literature Mary Simpson concludes:

"There is increasing evidence from a variety of studies that it is the structure and quality of the knowledge available to the individual which primarily determines the quality of his or her reasoning skills."[14]

McPeck makes the further point that philosophical and logical thinking is not sufficient in itself for the development of critical thinking. Logic is used to justify or detect fallacies in arguments and theories once they have been presented. But logic of itself cannot generate or formulate theories and new possibilities.

"In the most common problem solving situations within disciplines and working fields of knowledge... the most important phase is that of producing a hypothesis, conjecture or alternative that is worth checking or trying out".[15]

McPeck's position here is very similar to that of Peel. The exercise of imagining possibilities, coming up with suggestions and alternative explanations is fundamental to the development of critical thinking. It is this, among other things, that lies behind sub-element 2 of evaluating in Standard Grade Religious Studies: 'stating or explaining the implications of a concept, practice or viewpoint'.

Laying the foundations

The process of learning to evaluate, to form opinions and make judgements consists of a whole range of related skills, both cognitive and affective. This will be particularly the case at primary level where the foundations need to be laid for later development. If students are to work out the implications of holding a particular belief or following a particular practice; if they are to develop the ability to take account of number of factors and justify a conclusion by means of a developed argument, then much preparatory work must be done. The following would seem to be important in primary:

• **Open-mindedness** The development of an open-minded approach to knowledge and learning is fundamental to the development of critical thinking. I have already discussed the wider importance of this approach in the chapter on learning. Suffice it to say here that students from early primary need to be discouraged from regarding every question they come across as having only one single correct answer. Instead they need to be encouraged to go on thinking, to hypothesise and suggest new possibilities. If children are to develop such an attitude they need to be encouraged to examine their own ideas and actions, to be open to the ideas and opinions of others, and to accept the possibility that they might be wrong. They need to be encouraged also to draw their own conclusions, whatever these might be.

• **Imagining possibilities.** We saw in the work of Fowler that in the Mythic-Literal stage, with the onset of concrete operational thinking, the potential was present for children to look ahead and anticipate outcomes, provided they were addressing a concrete situation. This can be done, for example, by stimulating discussion in response to a range of stories suitable for Religious, Moral and Social Education. Children can be challenged with questions such as:
- what would have happened if...?
- what would you have done?
- what do you think?
- what do you think happened next?
Many of their theories will of course be weak or illogical. I recall a particular situation while driving with my own children. A police car overtook us at great speed with siren blaring and lights flashing, prompting my eight year old to remark, "Oh, there must be an accident somewhere" At which point my younger son, who had just turned five years old, exclaimed, "Perhaps the policeman's late for his lunch!" With sufficient stimulation and practice, however, children can be helped to improve their ability to theorise and predict outcomes.

• **Expressing and justifying opinions.** Students need at the very least to see the importance of supporting their opinions with reasons if they are to progress by the end of secondary to the more advanced skill of weighing up different viewpoints and deciding between their relative merits. Teachers often make the point to me that their students are quick to express their opinion but many don't seem able to justify it. This a major element in learning to evaluate. We are not born with an ability to support our opinions with evidence and argument. This has to be learned. We should be aiming here to bring most children, between the ages seven and eleven, to a level where they can express an opinion and justify it by articulating a straightforward reason. As Peel's research confirms some pupils may not learn to evaluate to any great extent. This means that we cannot ask children to evaluate the 'reasons for and against belief in God'. But we can ask them to consider different views about God as seen through the eyes of someone about their age.

In a recent book for children the idea of God is explored in a way which offers a useful introduction to the concept.[16] The central character, China, is sure there must be some kind of God somewhere and joins a scheme for the young to help old people. She meets Mr. Jupiter and strange events occur in the neighbourhood when he starts working his inventions. When he mysteriously disappears he leaves changes for the better. China and her friends wonder if they had imagined it all until they find Mr. Jupiter's toaster:

> "China took her toaster and placed it right in the middle of her top shelf, in the place of honour between the Pirate Bear and the Magic Book. And there it stayed, for ever afterwards: the toaster that saved the world.
> "You see, I tidied up, Mr.," whispered China.
> "You don't mind if I call you Mr. from now on, do you? Only God is such a frightening kind of word, and I think I know now that you're not really frightening at all.
> "Anyway, thanks a million for making it all right. And I hope you're OK now, wherever you are. I wish you could've stayed, but I know you had to go. But I just wanted to say that I'm really going to miss you. Goodbye Mr. and amen."

Among the questions children might be asked about this story are:
- what did China believe about Mr. Jupiter?
- why did she believe this?
- what other explanations are there?
- what did you think of Mr. Jupiter?
- what do you think God might be like?

• **Empathy.** Empathy or the ability to see and experience the point of view of others is crucial to the development of evaluation. Without the skill of appreciating what others have to say we cannot reach or sustain a balanced viewpoint on even straightforward issues. There are a number of ways in which we can encourage children to see things from another point of view, for example, through stories, role play and discussion. A story such as Roald Dahl's 'The Magic Finger' provides opportunities for a range of activities designed to help children see life from a different perspective.[17] The main character is an eight year old girl who, when angry, has the amazing power of being able to point her finger at people and cause all sorts of strange things happen to them. The Gregg family, who live next door, like to hunt and shoot animals and birds and this makes the little girl particularly cross. One day she points her magic finger at them and slowly they grow wings and are able to fly. At first they are excited to experience what it feels like to be a bird. Later, they become hungry and frightened as they find it difficult to get food and are threatened by hunters.

• **Self-awareness.** We have already discussed the importance of developing

self-awareness by halping students to reflect on their own beliefs and values in relation to teaching for personal development. Themes or topics on 'Myself' at early primary are commonplace within Religious and Moral Education or Environmental Studies. Opportunities for children to focus on themselves can help them to gain valuable insights into their own lives and to view themselves more objectively. A book such as 'Charlotte's Web' by E.B. White can be the starting point for writing, drawing, drama and discussion on the themes of friendship, loneliness, sadness and growing up.[18] The story centres on the relationship betwen an eight year old girl called Fern, a piglet called Wilbur, a rat called Templeton, and Charlotte the spider. Among the more important questions which emerge here are:
- what makes me happy/sad?
- what is most important to me?
- what helps me feel secure?
- why am I different?
- whom do I trust most?
- who are my real friends? [19]

Evaluating in the Secondary School

As we have already seen Standard Grade is underpinned by a system of Grade Related Criteria, which try to set out what candidates should know and be able to do before an award can be given. Grade Related Criteria or descriptions of performance are stated for three levels of achievement, Foundation, General and Credit, with Credit being the most demanding. These criteria provide realistic targets towards which teachers and students can work. Within Standard Grade we have said that evaluation consists of two dimensions or sub-elements.
These are:
1. considering the implications of religious concepts, practices and viewpoints for the individual and society today.
2. expressing and justifying an opinion on religious and moral issues.[20]
These, I believe, reflect Peel's understanding of what is involved in making judgements as well as the experience in Scotland of setting questions for the Ordinary Grade Religious Studies. In the following pages I have set out the criteria for evaluating in ascending order to show more clearly the progression from one level to another(see Table 1). Also included are the sub-elements of evaluating together with the corresponding criteria for each of the levels. In addition there are some sample questions which have been used to test each of the criteria. These are taken from Standard Grade Trial examinations given to candidates over the two successive years, 1989 and 1990. Finally, I have given a few examples to show the development across the levels making use of the same aspect of the same religion (see Table 2).

TABLE 1

Sub-element 1
Considering the implications of religious concepts, practices and viewpoints
for the individual and society today.

CREDIT

The candidate can give a developed explanation of a range of implications of a concept, practice or viewpoint.

GENERAL

The candidate can explain several implications of a concept, practice or viewpoint.

FOUNDATION

The candidate can state one or two straightforward implications of a concept, practice or viewpoint.

What temptations do you think the Church faces in continuing the ministry of Jesus today?

What effect might belief in samsara and karma have on how Hindus lead their lives?

What benefits and difficulties are there in accepting the language of the Incarnation as poetic rather than literal?

How does the idea of the resurrection help or hinder belief in Jesus today?

Muslims believe that God is 'Ruler of the Day for Repayment'. State two ways in which believing this might affect the way Muslims live their everyday lives.

In the passage, Muhammad is referred to as God's messenger. What do you consider are the main difficulties facing someone who claims to be a messenger of God?

Muslims believe that God is 'Judge'. Suggest one way in which this belief might affect how a Muslim leads his/her life.

Jewish parents like to include their children in the celebration of festivals. Suggest two ways in which this might benefit the children.

Sub-element 2
Expressing and justifying an opinion on religious and moral issues

CREDIT

GENERAL

FOUNDATION

The candidate can draw an appropriate conclusion on a complex issue and justify it by means of a developed argument based on a range of evidence and/or alternative viewpoints.

The candidate can express a coherent opinion on an issue and support it with several valid reasons.

In response to an issue or aspect of an issue, presented in straightforward terms, the candidate can offer an opinion, supported by one or two valid reasons.

Many Hindus believe the caste system to be fair. Do you agree or disagree? Give reasons for your answer.

The most important aspect of Islam is the submission of the believer to God. How far do you agree with this statement?

"So they hurried off and found Mary and Joseph and saw the baby lying in the manger. When the shepherds saw them they told them what the angel had said about the child". People understand this passage in different ways. Here are some of them.
A. This is part of a story told to show that Jesus is unique.
B. This is part of a story which has little meaning today.
C. This is not just a story but an event which happened as described.

Which do you think is the best one? Write A or B or C in the box and give a reason for your answer.

The idea of someone rising from the dead is impossible. Do you agree or disagree? Give reasons for your answer.

Which is more valuable for Jews, worship in the synagogue or worship in the home? Give reasons for your answer.

Can religious experience ever prove the truth of religious claims?

People who are totally opposed to war and believe that all disputes should be settled by peaceful means are called 'pacifists'. How far do you see 'pacifism' as the only moral response to the threat of war?

TABLE 2

Sub-element 1
Considering the implications of religious concepts, practices and viewpoints for the individual and society today.

Foundation	General	Credit
Muslims believe that God is Judge. Suggest ONE way in which this might affect how a Muslim leads his or her life.	Muslims beleive that God is 'Ruler of the Day of Repayment'. How might such a belief affect the way Muslims live their everyday lives?	"The destiny of every creature is already known to Allah." Discuss the implications of this statement for Muslim belief in God.

Sub-element 2
Expressing and justifying an opinion on religious and moral issues.

Foundation	General	Credit
"Suddenly the Lord stood among them" Why might people today find it difficult to believe that Jesus rose from the dead? Give TWO reasons for your answer.	Does the idea of the Resurrection help or hinder belief in Jesus today? Give reasons for your answer.	How far is it necessary or important for Christians to believe in the 'physical' resurrection of Jesus?

As part of evaluating in Standard Grade Religious Studies then students are expected to express and justify their opinions over a range of religious and moral issues. As we have seen, only at Credit level are they required to provide a developed argument by drawing conclusions based on a weighing of alternatives. And as we noted in the last section, Peel's research into the nature of adolescent judgement has shown that students experience great difficulty in dealing with problems and issues involving the selection and elimination of alternatives. These difficulties have been very much reflected in the performance of candidates in recent religious studies examinations in Scotland.

In the first 'pilot' examination in May 1988, the performance of candidates on evaluation questions was poor across all three levels. There were a number of reasons for this. Firstly, teachers had concentrated quite rightly on ensuring that they covered the content of the course. Activities therefore tended to be directed towards improving knowledge and understanding. Secondly, teachers were uncertain about how to develop students' ability to evaluate and about how much time should be spent doing this. Time spent developing skills, it was initially thought, was time taken from covering content. Perhaps some argued we should make sure of the content and then tackle evaluation. Thirdly, unlike knowledge and understanding which had to be grasped at each stage of the course, the ability to evaluate might be expected to improve over time as students obtained more practice. A year later evaluation, at least at Foundation and General levels showed a marked improvement. Pupils who were clearly struggling to recall correct information were doing well on those questions which required them to justify their opinions. Problems still existed, however, at credit level where candidates appeared to be finding difficulty with most questions. When answering questions which required looking at both sides of an issue, candidates frequently failed to do so, and instead gave reasons for preferring one side or the other. For example, having been asked to explain two ways in which people have tried to resolve the problem of suffering and evil, candidates had to choose one of these ways and say how far they saw it as a satisfactory explanation. One candidate who used the idea of suffering and evil as a punishment wrote:

"I find this explanation very unsatisfactory. If suffering is a punishment for sin why is it that completely innocent people suffer, e.g. thousands of people are killed each year from natural disasters. Surely they could not all have sinned so bad that they all deserved to be killed. And why are so many innocent people murdered each year. Surely it is the criminal who should suffer not the innocent victims. If suffering is a punishment why is it that so many bad people seem to do well often by cheating and hurting others."

A few candidates had succeeded, however, in mastering the art after only a year of the course. When asked to comment on whether religious experience could ever prove the truth of religious claims, one wrote:

"No, religious experience can't. Firstly the experience might be an hallucination or illusion created by the mind, and might never actually have occurred. People might lie or falsify reports for fame or money. They may attempt to con people by using experiences in which they believe God has spoken to them. Take an out-of-body experience in which the person claims to have floated out from their body and witnessed attempts to revive them. The person may claim to have gone along a tunnel of light and seen God. This could have been a reaction from the brain due to lack of oxygen, or it could have been something remembered from a film or documentary. However the person who has had the experience is the only person who can believe it. It can prove that God exists to the recipient of the experience as it seems reasonable to trust many of the things which happen to us. But this cant be used as hard evidence by others."[21]

This candidate has produced a developed argument based on a range of evidence to show that there are many difficulties associated with religious experience. At the same time he or she has recognised that there is another side to the question by pointing out that generally we have to trust most of our experiences. The candidate ends by eliminating this side of the issue on the grounds that this fact cannot be used as evidence by others.

On a series of occasions I asked teachers in the schools which I visited what they were specifically doing to help their pupils learn to evaluate. I received as you might expect a range of replies and have listed them below in their order of popularity:

- question and answer sessions with the whole class;
- encouraging pupils to discuss their ideas with each other before writing answers to questions;
- writing their own answers to evaluative questions;
- discussion with groups led by the teacher;
- structured discussion in groups with recording and reporting back;
- class debate.

From the list it is clear that question and answer sessions with the whole class were by far the most frequently used method. Where the teacher used these sessions to raise issues arising from the content, drawing attention to alternative explanations and possibilities for students to consider, they undoubtedly proved very effective. One such example was within a lesson on Hindu Gods. The teacher was showing slides which acted as the stimulus for discussing the nature and symbolism of the Hindu pantheon. Whenever the opportunity arose she would raise an issue with her students relating to Krishna's support of war or the advantages and disadvantages of believing in many Gods. This hopefully would not be the only occasion when her students confronted such issues, but it did represent an excellent beginning.

In the later stages of the course, teachers, in almost all the twenty one schools I visited, encouraged students to discuss their ideas with others in their group before writing answers to questions. This was frequently a valuable exercise although in discussion with pupils I have found it to be patchy. Sometimes "discussion" consisted of one pupil saying to another, "what did you get for question 2?" Although on occasions this in itself could be the starter for a much longer dialogue. With guidance from the teacher and practice on the part of pupils this activity can serve as a valuable addition to a varied methodology. Because the examination at the end of the course is a written one it is important that pupils get practice in writing their own answers to evaluative questions. This also gives the teacher the opportunity to assess how pupils are progressing. It is to the area of assessment that I now wish to turn.

NOTES AND BIBLIOGRAPHY

1   Sue Townsend *The Growing Pains of Adrian Mole* Methuen 1984
2   Quoted by Dr. Richard Jones, *Times Educational Supplement* 2.10.87
3   R. Goldman *Religious Thinking from Childhood to Adolescence* RKSP 1962, p62
4   Nicola Slee, 'Goldman Yet Again', in BJRE, Spring 1986
5   'Exploring Life', Lothian Regional Council, 1988, p.13
6   E.A. Peel *The Nature of Adolescent Judgement* Staples Press, 1971, p26
7   ibid p35
8   ibid p115
9   John Greer, BJRE, Spring 1984
10 See the article by W.D. Robinson in BJRE, Spring 88
11 Robinson, op.cit. p80
12 T. Jenkins, 'Philosophy for Children', in 'Values', Vol 2, no 3
13 John Mcpeck, Critical Thinking and Education, 1981,
14 Mary Simpson and Brian Arnold, 'Readings on Learning Difficulties in Secondary School Science', Northern College of Education, 1986, p.80
15 McPeck, op.cit. p15
16 Sue Limb *China Lee* Orchard, 1987
17 Roald Dahl *The Magic Finger* Puffin, 1974
18 E.B. White *Charlotte's Web* Puffin, 1963
19 For other ways of helping children to think critically, see Robert Fisher *Teaching Children to Think* Basil Blackwell, 1990
20 Standard Grade Arrangements for Religious Studies, 1989
21 Student responses are taken from candidates who sat the pilot examinations in 1989 and 1988; with the permission of the Scottish Examination Board.

7 ASSESSMENT AND EXAMINATIONS

Discusses some key issues in assessment such as formative versus summative, and norm-referenced versus criterion-referenced. The importance of assessment for learning is emphasised and a model for implementing diagnostic assessment is outlined, based on recent research. A comparison is made between the intention and format of questions in the Scottish 'O' Grade with those in the Standard Grade and GCSE.

ISSUES IN ASSESSMENT

"It is impossible for a teacher not to assess his pupils, and it would be wrong of him to refrain from doing so. All that is in question is the kind of assessment most helpful to teacher and to taught."[1]

Although small pockets of resistance undoubtedly still exist, the body of professional RE teachers seems wholeheartedly committed to the notion of improving assessment in religious education. In Scotland HM Inspectorate has reported that a growing number of schools with specialist teachers include religious education in the assessment arrangements for secondary years one and two. Unfortunately such practices were not continued in secondary years three and four to the same extent, except where certificate work was being done.[2] The remarks of HM Inspectors applied mainly to those assessments which take place at the end of school terms and form the basis of report cards. Little was said about the more informal assessments which take place as part of students' learning.

Formative/Diagnostic

This informal kind of assessment is usually called formative or diagnostic assessment. It is designed to encourage and improve students' learning in the classroom in three main ways:
1 by identifying and correcting students' weaknesses and misunderstandings;
2. by helping to determine the level of tasks students should do next;
3. by advising students on what to concentrate their efforts.
These assessments might take the form of comments on classwork or homework exercises. They might also be focussed on group activities. For

example, a teacher is going round groups listening in to discussions on the advantages and disadvantages of arranged marriages. The teacher might encourage students to develop certain aspects of the topic by saying, "that's a good point, what does the rest of the group think about that". She might ask a particular individual to expand on an opinion they have expressed by giving a reason. Or she might want to encourage them to look at an area which they have not yet considered by saying, "OK, now what about looking at it from the point of view of the parents?" On occasions, while listening to a group discussion, the teacher may want to say more in order to help students clarify and articulate their ideas, clear up misconceptions, add new information, as well as point students in the direction of relevant resources. This practice of listening and responding to students' talk is a vital aspect of formative assessment, and one in which all teachers can engage. The only requirement is that some variety in teaching approaches be introduced to allow students some opportunity to work as a group or as individuals. In addition to student talk other sources of formative assessment are assignments, worksheets to complete at home or in class, or a report of a discussion or visit. These exercises arise directly out of the learning process and are often preferable to specially created tests since they assess as closely as possible what has just been learned.

There has been in recent years a significant rise in the importance of formative assessment. Although the Standard Grade Review of Assessment Group in Scotland (SGROAG) was mainly concerned with assessment in relation to national certification, it was nevertheless insistent that:

> "...assessment should form an integral part of the learning and teaching process, more for its ability to indicate success in coping with day-to-day demands, and for the part it might play in identifying weaknesses, than for the contribution it makes to final certification."[3]

Within the National Curriculum, the Task Group on Assessment and Testing (TGAT) did not consider the boundary between formative and diagnostic assessment as at all clear and recommended that:

> "...the basis of of the national system be essentially formative, but designed also to indicate where there is need for more detailed diagnostic assessment. At age 16, however, it should incorporate assessment with summative functions."[4]

Formative/Summative

As in the two reports just mentioned, formative is usually seen alongside summative assessment, the distinction being not in the form of assessment but in the intentions of the assessor. In other words, is the assessment being used to improve a student's learning? If so, formative. Or is the intention to obtain information about a student's present progress and report it to a third party, parents or potential employers? If so, summative. The boundary between formative annd summative, however, is not always clear-cut. Clearly an examination at the end of a course for the purpose of certification is summative. A teacher's comments on a piece of research being undertaken by a student with a view to that student producing the best possible end-product is certainly formative. But what about an end of term or end of unit test. This may provide the teacher with information regarding the student's progress and in addition, through discussion with the student, help him or her to improve their performance in the unit which follows. This is particularly appropriate where similar skills of investigation and evaluation are being practised in successive units. This dual purpose of assessment raises an important question for teachers. If both the summative and formative purposes of assessment are important, how are teachers to organise their time so as to include both? The answer lies in keeping summative assessment to a minimum, while expanding the use of assessment as a formative and diagnostic tool. I shall return to this point in the next section. But to complete the present discussion, the following contexts for assessment are examples of what might be used for both formative and summative purposes:

- investigating an issue or an aspect of an issue
- writing a report on a group discussion
- test with a range of questions increasing in difficulty
- writing a report on a survey or interview
- selecting and commenting on the content of a TV programme
- writing a report for a newspaper
- imaginative writing
- preparing a tape of a group discussion.

Continuous/Terminal

Another on-going debate within assessment relates to whether a student should be assessed from time to time throughout a course or whether he or she is to be assessed only at the end of it, that is, continuous assessment or terminal assessment. Obviously the length and nature of such a course will make a considerable difference to the significance of this debate. In a short course or forty hour module where the aim is to get as many students as possible up to a defined minimum standard, terminal assessment will need to take place about three quarters of the way through the course. This gives time for remedial action to be taken for those who have not attained the criteria at the first attempt. It is likely that other earlier assessments will have a formative purpose. In courses which are spread over a longer period or within linked courses, teachers will want more frequent summative assessments to take place at least at the end of each term's work. Sometimes the results of such summative assessments will be reported to parents. Despite the frequency of such assessments teachers involved have not generally regarded this as continuous assessment. This is probably because, as Rowntree points out, the debate "is not really between continuous and terminal assessment at all" but "between continuous and terminal grading".[5] The debate is really about whether the continuous assessment, which may be taking place anyway, should actually count towards the final grade. It is about whether the final grade should depend solely on a "big bang" examination or whether previous assessments should also be taken into account. Finally it can also be about the degree of influence teachers should have in determining grades for their pupils within a national system of assessment. Both the new Scottish Standard Grade system and GCSE offer interesting combinations of continuous and terminal grading. In Standard Grade, for example, teachers must arrive at an estimate grade for each candidate for each element or domain to be assessed. These estimates are subsequently compared with the actual grades achieved by the candidates in the written examination, before a final grade is awarded. In GCSE it is the continuous grading of coursework which contributes to students' final grades.

Norm-referenced/Criterion-referenced

Most teachers are familiar with an approach to grading which begins with a predetermined distribution across the range of grades. Using grades A B C D and E, for example, teachers will expect to award about 10 A's, 20 B's, 40 C's, 20 D's and 10 E's for every 100 students who sit the test. The assumption being made here is that we cannot expect all students to achieve a worthwhile level of attainment. Therefore only a few will do very well, the majority will be average, and a few will do badly. This approach to grading and assessment is known as norm-referenced, that is, the student is being judged according to how well he has done compared with the norm established by his fellow students. Tests prepared within such a system will indicate who does best and who worst. Some will score very well, while others, usually those who are already experiencing learning difficulties, will score badly or even nothing at all. Difficult questions will be included so as to discriminate between the good and not so good candidates and question setters will exclude questions that too many students would get right. As a result we will not, except by implication, be able to tell much about what a particular student actually knows or can do. It has been largely this view, that such information about an individual's abilities is important, which has led in recent years to the change from norm- referenced to criterion-referenced assessment. Criterion-referencing is about judging the student according to how well he has done compared with some pre-determined criterion.

One of the earliest discussions of criterion-referencing in Scotland occurs in the Dunning report where we read:

> "the specification of the standard of attainment for each award should refer to criteria detailed in the subject guidelines and should not depend on grading pupils relative to one another."[6]

It was criterion referencing that Dunning recommended for the bulk of internal testing particularly that which was intended for formative purposes. Criterion referencing seems to be most effective when applied to the testing of specific learning objectives related to particular pieces of work. Examples of students' work can be looked at in relation to appropriate criteria and a decision made as to whether the criteria have been met. Problems arise, however, when attempts are made to group such information together and arrive at a conclusion regarding a student's understanding of a unit or a whole course. Having commissioned a number of research projects into criterion-referencing, the Scottish Education Department concluded:

"that much has yet to be learned before it would be possible to make criterion-referenced techniques the sole basis on which certification can take place."[7]

Affective

Religious Education teachers have long been concerned about learning and assessing within the affective area. The affective includes such phenomena as interests, attitudes, appreciations, values and emotions. At a basic level teachers understand the importance of students possessing a willingness to learn. Engaging students actively through a variety of learning approaches and relating content to their own experience of life are among some of the more important ways of promoting this willingness. Some teachers fear, however, that with the current emphasis on the acquisition of cognitive skills within new examinations, religious studies will focus only on those aspects which are most susceptible to external certification. Certainly such "elements" as knowledge, understanding, evaluation, and investigation do not exhaust the range of outcomes which teachers may consider important to a sound religious education.

The assessment of affective characteristics is not without its problems. If this were not the case, we would see much more of it going on in both school-based and national assessments. The most common way in which teachers have been seen to introduce affective assessment is through the provision of a descriptive comment on report cards in addition to grades. These comments frequently make reference to things like degree of effort, enthusiasm for the subject and behaviour in the classroom. The trouble with these is that they are just as likely to be revealing information about the state of classroom learning, not to mention the teacher, as about the student. Also there is unlikely to be much agreement between teachers on the rating of student attitudes. Different teachers will develop different perceptions of the same student depending on the nature of the relationship between them, as well as on the student's likes or dislikes of a particular activity or subject. Within the 16-18 development programme in Scotland it was decided that attitudes would not be assessed and reported on in the same way as cognitive abilities.

The most important reason given for this was that these attitudes would be difficult to measure because "the tests would be time consuming to administer and inaccurate in result."[8] A similar position has been adopted within the National Curriculum where the assessment of attitudes is not to be a prescribed part of the national assessment system.

An important question therefore is how assessments in this area can be made more accurate. One way is to make such assessments and reports descriptive rather than judgemental. Dockrell describes a study in which teachers were asked to write down examples of behaviour which they believed represented 'effort' on a scale of 1 to 6. These were subsequently discussed, reviewed and eventually rewritten until an agreed list was established. These behaviours had to be descriptions of behaviour rather than judgements such as "wastes time by talking". These agreed examples of 'effort' then provided the basis for teacher assessment.[9] Some teachers and schools will prefer not to indicate levels, in which case descriptions of typical behaviour could be devised across a limited number of aspects. Teachers would then select from these and copy them on to reports or profiles. Studies indicate that teachers appear to be concerned mainly with what might be termed 'perseverance' and 'enterprise'. This appears to be the case even when a large number of assessments is made.
     "Increasing the apparent range of assessments does not increase the range of aspects of pupils actually reported."[10]

Among the affective characteristics encouraged by many religious education courses are certain emotional and moral attitudes. Important among these would be things like ' willingness to put oneself in the position of others' and 'concern for others and desire to promote their welfare'. The first might be assessed informally through teacher observation of student group discussions or through some form of self-assessment. Among the criteria for judgement could be the following:
- does the student listen to other points of view?
- does he/she agree with other peoples' suggestions?
- does he/she build on other peoples' ideas?
- is he/she prepared to change his/her mind if proved wrong?
These criteria represent only the beginnings of empathy as an element in greater understanding. Yet without such willingness to at least consider and appreciate the ideas and opinions of others, there seems little chance of students ever becoming more sensitive and responsive to the beliefs and ways of life of people who are different from themselves. Self-assessment might also be useful in relation to students' developing concern for others. Students could indicate features of their activities which relate to showing concern in an active way. This might take the form of a weekly diary and include activities both inside and outside school. Or it might be done by means of a given checklist which students tick or underline before proceeding to give

more details of what they had done and why. These kinds of exercises should be an integral part of learning and teaching. If the information resulting from them is to be used within student profiles then comments should be descriptive rather than judgemental.

ASSESSMENT FOR LEARNING

In a survey of schools it was found that 42% of middle schools and 51% of secondary schools had writen policies on assessment. One third of all the schools in the sample had no existing written policy at all on assessment. From those schools which sent in supporting documentation it was clear that policies were mostly concerned with establishing a grading system which could operate across all subjects. According to the authors of the survey such grading systems were easily classified into two types:

> "a five-point scale of ability and attainment or a five-point scale of ability together with a similar scale for effort."[11]

This norm-referenced system is seen by many to have two major drawbacks. First, it provides little useful information about what students are actually achieving. Second, it does nothing to improve motivation which is often particularly low among the less able.

As a result many schools have now moved away from grading each subject on an A to E scale of attainment and reporting these grades on a single report sheet. Instead, a report sheet or profile is provided for each subject allowing a good deal more information about students to be included. Teachers' comments can be more comprehensive and assessment is generally criterion-referenced, with each subject producing broad statements of achievement which are then applied to a number of elements within the subject. For example, the following report sheet is intended for first year secondary and includes a description of the course. The descriptions of performance on the left apply to the elements of assessment, and the numbered items on the right apply to Homework, Effort and Behaviour.[12]

COURSE RELIGIOUS EDUCATION

COURSE DESCRIPTION
Pupils are introduced to the principal beliefs and practices of the world's major religious traditions through the study of six themes namely community, story, people, celebration, communication and values. These themes are studied in four contexts: the home and family; the local community; the plural community and the global community.

ELEMENTS OF ASSESSMENT

Knowledge   Homework
Understanding   Effort
Evaluation   Behaviour
Skills

1 Demonstrates a thorough grasp of all the   1   Excellect
  areas covered.   2   Good
2 Copes well with most of the areas   3   Satisfactory
  covered.   4   Causing concern
3 Can cope with the basic work required.   5   Unsatisfactory
4 Has difficulty in coping with the basic
  work given.
N Not possible to assess at this stage.

COMMENT

Such developments avoid making unfair comparisons between students on the basis of overall grades. Instead there is an attempt to show what students can do in relation to different aspects of a subject by relating grades to positive descriptions of performance. In the future these description are likely to reflect more closely the criteria for Standard Grade and 5-14 developments in Scotland, and the key stages of the National Curriculum in England. For example, the following elements of a student profile, incorporating descriptions of performance at three levels, would be appropriate for early secondary.

PUPIL PROFILE

	3	2	1
Knowledge	can state some basic facts about...	can select and present factual knowledge in an organised way	can select and present factual knowledge in a well organised way and with attention to detail
Understanding	can give a simple explanation of the meaning or importance of...	can explain clearly the meaning or significance of... with some attention to detail	can explain the meaning or significance of... and relationships betweem... with considerable clarity and insight
Evaluation	can express a personal opinion and support it with at least one reason	can express an opinion and justify it clearly and coherently	can articulate an opinion and back it with supportive argument
Co-operation	needs some encouragement when operating as a member of a group	participates will in a group and can accept responsibility	participates well and can take the lead in involving others
Investigating	needs considerable help in finding, selecting and presenting relevant information	with some help can research information from several sources and present it	shows considerable independence as a researcher and communicator of information from a variety of sources
Self-Assessment	needs help in assessing own performance	can assess own performance without help	can assess own performance and make suggestions about improvement.

Models of teaching assessment

Any attempt, however, to emphasise the positive nature of students' performances must start in the classroom with the learning process itself. In the survey referred to above the authors claimed it was rare to find within any school policy a reference to the different purposes of assessment, in particular relating to assessment as an integral part of teaching and learning. In a similar survey in Scotland only 29% of schools had a policy relating to this aspect of assessment.[13] There seems little point in reporting what students can do in a positive way if learning and teaching within the classroom is not geared to improving the learning of all students. This not only means a variety of learning and teaching approaches, coupled with appropriate differentiation, but also formative and diagnostic assessment. Diagnostic assessment is a type of formative assessment since both are intended as a means of improving students' learning. Diagnostic assessment, however, is more specifically directed towards identifying and putting right students' weaknesses and misunderstandings.

The most widely researched approach to assessment as part of teaching is that associated with Benjamin Bloom.[14] He advocates a form of 'mastery learning' and diagnostic assessment to determine whether or not mastery has been achieved. He argues that all students will make better progress if they attain mastery of clearly specified intended outcomes at each stage of their learning. Provided students are given feedback and help when they have learning difficulties, and if they are given sufficient time to master each learning outcome, then results can be dramatic, claim Bloom and his associates. They also claim that students' motivation for learning will improve because they are being give frequent evidence of their successes. Underlying the approach is the idea that students should be allowed to master each sequential element of learning before moving on to the next. Bloom's approach has been applied mostly to simple reading and number development where sequence is clear and straightforward. There is little evidence so far of its successful application over a wider range of subject matter and skills.[15]

A more flexible model was devised by the Diagnostic Assessment Project, conducted by the Scottish Council for Research in Education and funded by the Scottish Education Department. This study, like others of its kind, arose from the deliberations of the Dunning Committee on Assessment in Scotland. The Committee stated that:

"Diagnostic tests enable teachers to gain detailed information on the particular points of difficulty for each pupil, information which is necessary if there is to be improvement of performance. In such tests the responses selected by pupils from a number of options can indicate that a certain concept or process has or has not been grasped. The subsequent

action is to select and offer alternative learning experiences to remedy the difficulties diagnosed."[16]
The project worked closely with teachers encouraging them to set their own learning outcomes which included higher order skills and affective outcomes as well as low level ones relating to recall and simple understanding. The researchers claim that the model is suitable for a wide variety of teaching styles and management situations provided that some time can be set aside for giving individual help to those who are experiencing difficulties. There are at least three stages in the development of such a model:[17]

(a) *Specifying learning outcomes*: These should cover the whole range of outcomes considered important in a religious studies course. This will involve outcomes relating to knowledge and understanding, evaluation as well as affective outcomes. End of course examinations specialise in sampling from large scale domains such as 'knowledge and understanding of key concepts and related sources and practices within Christianity'. In contrast, learning outcomes for diagnostic purposes will relate to small scale domains such as individual concepts and skills. For example, 'students should be able to give an explanation of what Christians mean by Kingdom of God' or 'students should express and justify an opinion on the issue of whether the exodus story owes more to legend than to history'. Intended outcomes for knowledge and understanding of particular parts of a course need to be mastered by students as far as possible before moving on to the next, since there is unlikely to be enough time to revisit them. Other outcomes such as the ability to evaluate are longitudinal in nature and will occur throughout the course. There is therefore less urgency in this case to test each and every learning outcome. This view, however needs some qualification in that the particular context of evaluation can make a difference to students' ability to do well. For example, students may find it easier to evaluate moral issues rather than issues arising from beliefs within Islam or Judaism.

(b) *Introducing instruments of assessment*: There need be no restriction on the type of assessment instrument used for diagnostic purposes. The two essential requirements of good diagnostic tests are that they relate to areas or domains of knowledge that are manageable and appropriate, and that they test what they set out to test, that is that they are content valid. A range of techniques from short answer tests, through extended writing to reports on an investigation or group discussion would be suitable. Preferably these should function as constituent elements of the classwork and should be seen as such by students. The most important question is when should they be applied. Tests should be applied within the time span allotted to the specified learning outcomes so that provision can be made for reinforcement or extension work before the class moves on to a new section. The summary chart outlined in the following chapter is what I would have in mind here.

When teachers are satisfied, within given time restraints, that students have been given sufficient opportunity to achieve a particular learning outcome then diagnostic assessment can be applied.

(c) *Making use of the information provided*: The information gleaned from diagnostic assessment can be used in a variety of ways. Teachers can gain information about students' levels of attainment in relation to particular concepts, skills or elements of knowledge. This information can be used, for example, to make decisions about the use of differentiated work. Teachers can decide whether a particular student requires reinforcement at his or her current level or whether he or she would be more profitably engaged in a task which extends his or her knowledge and/or skills. A student who satisfactorily demonstrates the ability to understand the concept of resurrection, by providing an explanation of the concept with reference to the significant facts in the resurrection narrative, would be best employed finding out about the different ways in which Christians understand resurrection today.

On the other hand, a student may have failed to understand the relationship between the Christian practice of communion and Jesus' last meal with his disciples. This may have been due to a confusion with the Jewish passover meal in which, according to the story, Jesus and his disciples were participating. Or it may have been caused by the way it was presented by the teacher, or both. In which case a short discussion with the teacher may be the best way of remedying this. Other common misunderstandings relate to the concept Incarnation, the significance of which is frequently seen as being 'the birth of Jesus'. Students often see the reason for giving presents at Christmas in the gifts of the wise men to the baby Jesus, rather than in God's gift of his Son to humankind. Students studying Hinduism alongside Christianity often confuse incarnation with reincarnation.

Teachers might also use the information to find out whether any of their intended outcomes are proving too difficult for the class as a whole. If so they will need to reconsider their objectives for future years. If the learning outcome has emerged from long term aims or targets within an examination syllabus it may be trying to encompass too large an area of content and need to be reduced. The problem may also reflect a difficult area of the syllabus which requires more time spent on it.

Diagnosing students' difficulties

The job of pin-pointing actual learning problems which students have is certainly made easier by the existence of clear attainment targets and performance statements. For example, if primary teachers know that an important target in religious education is concerned with helping children "develop a knowledge of the ways in which people celebrate, and an understanding of the concept of celebration and the values and attitudes being expressed"; and if they also know that most children, by the time they are aged eleven, (Key Stage Two of the National Curriculum, 7-11 years) should have gone some way towards attaining this target by demonstrating that they are:

(a)   able to describe the main features of the celebration of different festivals;

(b)   able to relate the story associated with a festival to the actual celebration and to the feelings being expressed on the occasion;

(c)   familiar with ways in which a fast is observed;[18]

then they can design initial learning experiences to ensure the satisfactory progress of all children, and provide additional help for those who are having difficulties.

Classroom tests, followed by revision exercises or extra homework, however, may not be sufficient here. Such procedures do not take account of the possibility that the source of difficulty may lie outside the topic area within previous learning or within students commonsense understandings. Simpson and Arnold argue that diagnosing students' learning difficulties is a two stage process. The first involves the use of class tests referenced to performance statements in order to identify the area of failure. This might be a particular concept or skill or item of knowledge. Remediation takes the form of additional work relating to the area of difficulty. The second involves activities designed to discover the cause of student learning difficulty. Many of the learning difficulties experienced by students, they say, are traceable either to a failure occurring in earlier learning or to inadequacies in the structure and presentation of material currently being taught.[19] Since routine tests and assignments are unlikely to reveal the nature of students' prior knowledge, or indeed the quality of teachers' presentation, Simpson and Arnold used interviews with open-ended questions to investigate students' understanding of concepts. They concluded: "As a result of our experience we regard listening to pupil talk as the most important single diagnostic activity of teachers."[20]

Grading and Recording

There is a genuine concern among teachers that they can end up spending too much time testing. The practice of encouraging students to assess themselves can go a long way towards reducing the overall burden on teachers. Information from the results of formative assessment can contribute to summative reports. For example, summative grades could be supplemented by descriptive comments on strengths and weaknesses of students gleaned from successive formative assessments. Since this demands some form of record to be kept of the process of learning, a diary can be kept primarily by students themselves. In it they could be invited to say whether they found particular tasks easy or difficult and why, as well as commenting on areas they found especially interesting. Alternatively a checklist might be used by students themselves to record their achievements. The following questions might form the basis of such a checklist in relation to understanding and evaluating an issue of belief or morality, for secondary pupils:

- Have you explained one or two viewpoints on the issue?
- Have you outlined some of the different aspects involved in the issue and explained clearly a number of opposing viewpoints?
- Have you outlined all the different aspects of the issue and given a full explanation of the different viewpoints?
- Have you stated your own opinion and supported it with one or two reasons?
- Have you expressed your opinion clearly and supported it with several reasons?
- Have you drawn your own conclusion based on the examination of arguments on both sides of the issue?

Some recording by teachers will, however, be essential on the way to determining a final grade for students at the end of a year or course. But how frequently ought we to record the results of such summative assessments? Certainly we want to avoid any tendency towards over assessment, towards attempting to grade every piece of work students complete in order to build up a complex profile for each student. On the other hand, we want to avoid basing grades on one isolated performance, for example, an end of term examination. This is unlikely to show the best of what our students know and can do. There is no reason why summative assessment cannot be linked closely with the day-to-day learning of students, by making normal classwork the focus of assessments. One advantage of this is that candidates' grades can be based on learning that has just taken place. In so far as effective learning does not involve retaining information over a long period, this will benefit students who have difficulty with this.

Normally students should be told in advance about assignments which are to be used primarily for grading purposes. This will serve to distinguish them from other purely formative or diagnostic assessment which may be going on in relation to work arising from the normal learning process. Such formative assessment is likely to be associated particularly with initial learning as well as reinforcement and revision work. This should enable students to see these assessments as specifically designed to help them to learn as opposed to assessment for grading which is likely to be a source of some concern. For example, Black and Dockrell reported a marked positive response to diagnostic assessment amongst students. Teachers felt that it helped students to admit to their problems and discuss them openly. There seemed to be much less anxiety among students about diagnostic assessment than there was about summative tests and examinations. As one student remarked: "Exams worry me because I think I'm going to forget everything. Tests worry me as much because they also go towards my final mark at the end of the year."[21]

In Standard Grade Religious Studies students must show knowledge and understanding of concepts, sources and practices, and demonstrate ability to evaluate issues across four units - Christianity, Issues of Belief, Issues of Morality, and one other world religion. Teachers are expected to provide an estimate grade at the end of the course for both knowledge and understanding and evaluation across these four units. One suggestion is that teachers assess each unit twice, once about half way through the unit and once near the end. This would make a total of eight occasions over the two year course. From this group of recorded grades teachers are expected to determine an overall grade supported by evidence in the form of students' work. This overall grade must represent sustained performance on the part of the student rather than a single exceptional performance which was never repeated. Grades achieved later in the course will normally be accorded more weight than those achieved earlier allowing students' developing abilities to be taken into account.

In GCSE Coursework it is the student's best performances which must be included in the determination of his or her overall grade. Examining Groups vary in the number of assignments required for coursework assessment. It is no easy matter to decide whether all students are best served by a large number of short assignments or a small number of longer assignments. Over a two year course students will complete many more short assignments than are required for summative asessment purposes. This should provide the teacher with sufficient material from which to select a student's best work. Teachers might be well advised to give students a good deal of practice in the early part of the course, using assessments formatively to improve students' performances. Summative assessments could then be concentrated in the latter part of the course. This is particularly important in relation to students' ability to evaluate which tends to improve as the course progresses. The precise balance of these, however, must lie with the teacher in relation to the particular course.[22] Longer assignments will inevitably be less frequent and there is therefore greater pressure on students to achieve their best performance on each of two or three occasions. Formative assessment of the kind outlined in the first section and opportunities to redraft initial work will help students to achieve their best performance.

Within general religious education, where time is at a premium, grades are likely to be based on short assignments. They might be based on a single performance or may be the result of a judgement made on several

performances completed either in class or for homework. If students are to
be given an opportunity to achieve the best grades possible, then that grade
should perhaps be based on assessments made in a variety of contexts. A
sample of work for grading purposes might contain, say, three items. For
example:

1   a small scale investigative task in which students are asked to not only
    demonstrate knowledge and understanding but also express an opinion
    supported by reasons or argument.
2   a written report on a group discussion. This will be particularly valuable
    for assessing students ability to evaluate.
3   a series of questions to test students knowledge and understanding and
    evaluation skills. Such a test should ideally consist of questions increasing
    in difficulty. If levels of criteria are available then these would form the
    basis of question difficulty.

All three assessment instruments could be used with all students and are
therefore particularly suitable for grading in the earlier part of a course,
before teachers have strong evidence of students' actual levels of performance.
In the latter stages of the course, differentiated tasks might also be included,
so that students have a variety of opportunities to show clearly what they
know, understand and can do.

As well as providing information about students' attainment levels for
grading purposes, these short assignments can also provide teachers with the
opportunity to do even more formative assessment. This will be particularly
appropriate where attainment targets are available. Teachers could comment
and make suggestions on students' drafts, giving them the opportunity to
improve their performance before grading takes place. There is no reason
why grades resulting from these assessments should only be recorded after a
student's first attempt. It may be that a particular students' class exercise or
piece of homework fell well below his or her usual level of performance and
should be done again before grading. Or it may be that students are
instructed to complete a first draft to be checked before handing it in for
inclusion as part of the sample for grading purposes. Between the first and
second gradings teachers can discuss with students their level of attainment.
By discussing students' work in relation to appropriate targets, teachers can
help students to improve their performance next time round.

Examinations

In May 1984 students in Scotland were able, for the first time, to present
themselves for an examination in Religious Studies certificated by the Scottish
Examination Board. Hitherto Scottish students who chose to do religious
studies had been presented for GCE examinations. The new Scottish "O"
Grade required candidates to answer questions from two sections,

Christianity and one other World Religion, selected from Hinduism, Islam and Judaism. There is a choice of questions and candidates are expected to answer five questions over two and a half hours, two from the first section, two from the second section, and one from either. Questions were of the structured variety each totalling 15 marks. The following examples are taken from recent "O" Grade papers:

1   (a) What promises are made by parents when they have their babies
        baptised?   3
    (b) Why might parents wish to have their babies baptised?   3
    (c) What factors might lead to parents not keeping the promises
        they make at the baptism of their baby?   3
    (d) How relevant for today are Christian teachings about
        relationships between parents and children?   6
                                                                              (15)

5   (a) What pilgrimage rites are performed at the Ka'ba?   3
    (b) Why is the Ka'ba the central shrine of Islam?   4
    (c) Describe what happens at the festival at the end of the Hajj.   3
    (d) How might a Muslim have his faith deepened by going on
        the Hajj?   5
                                                                              (15)

1   (a) In the Ramayana, what part is played by Hanuman?   3
    (b) Describe how this story is used as a theme in one popular
        Hindu festival.   4
    (c) Why do you think the Ramayana is widely used as a
        children's reading book in Indian schools?   3
    (d) How far could the modern Hindu teenager in Britain use
        the Ramayana themes or characters as ideal models?   5
                                                                              (15)

This format is typical of questions which have appeared in "O" grade examinations since 1984, although often they were introduced by a passage or illustration. They usually consisted of three or four parts with a relatively straightforward starter question demanding simple recall of information. The following one or two parts usually required more understanding and were more difficult. The general intention here, as in the former GCE examinations, was to discriminate between those candidates who could reach the required standard and those who could not. The final question was almost always an attempt to go beyond the knowledge demanded by the course content and ask candidates to make a judgement on an issue or comment on the relevance of a particular practice or belief. Unlike the new Standard Grade, however, teachers and students alike had no clear idea of what was expected in these questions. The Arrangements for the "O" Grade simply state that the objectives for the course include developing skills in evaluating arguments, drawing conclusions and applying insights. Nevertheless many students, and not just the more able performed well on these questions, presumably because answers did not depend wholly on the recall of specific information.

The following questions are taken from the Standard Grade examination given to pilot schools in May 1989. They are representative of all three levels, Foundation, General and Credit. Candidates answer questions from two adjacent levels, Foundation and General or General and Credit. The following questions are taken from Foundation, Hinduism; General, Christianity; and Credit, Islam.

FOUNDATION

> "The Blessed Lord said:
> Many a birth have I passed through,
> And [many a birth] hast thou:
> Thou knowest not."
> *Bhagavad Gita* 4:5

4 (a) Which of the following words means passing through many births? Tick the correct box.

DHARMA ☐

SAMSARA ☐

MOKSHA ☐   1

(b) The reason why a person passes through many births is because of KARMA.
What is KARMA?

_____
_____
_____
_____   4

(c)   Do you think it would be better to live only one life or to be reborn a number of times?
Tick a box and give one reason for your answer.

One life   ☐

Reborn many times   ☐

REASON:_____

_____

_____   2

GENERAL

1 (a)   The picture shows part of a service for Good Friday. Why do some Christians have special services on Good Friday?

_____

_____

_____   2

(b)   "If the story of Jesus ended on Good Friday, Christianity wouldn't be what it is today."
What difference does the resurrection make to how Christians understand the events of Good Friday?

_____

_____

_____

_____   3

(c)   In what ways is the resurrection of Jesus remembered in public worship?

_____

_____

_____

_____   3

(d)   "The idea of someone rising from the dead is impossible"
Do you agree or disagree? Give reasons for your answer.

_____

_____

_____

_____

_____

_____   6

CREDIT

    5 (a) Choose two of the many names for God. Explain in detail what
        they teach Muslims about the character of God?   4
    (b) Explain why Muslims forbid any pictorial representation
        of their God.   3
    (c) "The most important aspect of Islam is the submission
        of the believer to God."
        How far do you agree with this statement?   6

                                     (K, U, E)

Unlike the "O" Grade questions these questions do not intentionally contain
parts which vary in difficulty. Questions in each level of the examination
paper, Foundation, General and Credit should reflect the criteria for that
level and therefore, in theory, should represent the same level of difficulty. In
reality, however, many factors influence the difficulty of a question including
the wording, content, sequence of parts, as well as the emphasis given by the
teacher. As a result some candidates will perform better on a question at a
higher level than at a lower level. What is important, however, is that each
part of a question tests a specific criterion statement and that as a whole the
questions in each level clearly differentiate the relative demands of each level.
Although like the "O" Grade, questions are structured, there is a good deal
more variety in the type of question being asked. This is particularly true at
Foundation level where filling in the blanks and ticking boxes is much in
evidence. As we move up the levels towards General and Credit, questions
become more open with less support being given to candidates on how they
are to frame their answers. At all levels questions are clearly designated as
being knowledge/understanding or evaluation. Candidates are given a total
mark for each of these elements and subsequently a grade. At Foundation
and General levels candidates write their answers on the question papers,
while at Credit separate sheets are provided.

We have already noted that in GCSE Religious Studies differentiation is
based not on separate examination papers for different grades, as in Standard
Grade, but on a common paper covering all grades, with questions increasing
in difficulty. The following examples are taken from the Northern
Examining Association's Syllabus A, Paper 1, Christianity for May 1988.
Candidates must answer all questions in the paper. Questions are arranged
across three sections, A, B and C. Section A consists of short answer
questions requiring straightforward recall of information or simple
understanding.

For example:

A11   What is Advent?

_____
_____2

A12   Name two events in the life of Jesus which are particularly remembered
      during Epiphany.
1_____
2_____2

A13   What is the first day of Lent called?
_____1

A14   What event in the New Testament do Christians remember at Pentecost?
_____
_____2

A15   Why do some Christians say a dead person is at rest?
_____
_____
_____2

A16   Why do prayers often end with the word 'Amen'?
_____
_____
_____2

A17   What is liturgical worship?
_____
_____
_____2

Section B questions are structured questions introduced by a picture or
written stimulus, and including knowledge, understanding, and evaluation
elements. As in section A answers are to be written on the question papers.

For example:

B21   Read the following extract from the rock musical Jesus Christ Superstar.
          Nazareth your famous son should have stayed a great unlnown
          Like his father carving wood - he'd have made good
          Tables, chairs and oaken chests would have suited Jesus best
          He'd have caused nobody harm - no one alarm.

(a) (i) Who is meant by 'his father carving wood'?

_____   1

(ii) Why might many Christians object to this person being
described as 'the Father of Jesus'?

_____
_____
_____
_____3

(b) Which words from the Apostles' Creed show what Christians
believe about the birth of Jesus?

_____
_____
_____
_____3

(c) Here is the ending of Jesus Christ Superstar.
JESUS:
God forgive them - they don't know what they are doing.
Who is my mother? Where is my mother?
My God my God why have you forgotten me?
I am thirsty
It is finished
Father into you hands I commend my Spirit.

Why might a Christian think this was not a suitable place for an
account of the life of Jesus to end?

_____
_____
_____
_____4

(d) Do you think that a Musical is a suitable way to present the life
of Jesus?

_____
_____
_____
_____4

In section C greater demands are clearly being made on candidates both in
terms of understanding and evaluation. For these questions candidates must
write their answers on supplementary sheets.

For example:

C23 (a)   Why do Christians read and study the Bible?   5
     (b)   Some people say the Bible is not true.
         Say whether or not you agree with them. Give your reasons
         and use passages from the Bible to support your opinions.   10

C24   In this question, you may write about confirmation in **either** the
      Roman Catholic or the Anglican Church.
     (a)   At about what age are young people usually confirmed?
         Why is this age considered suitable?   3
     (b)   What do those who are being confirmed promise?
         Give one other occasion when similar promises are made.   5
     (c)   At a confirmation service the candidates are confirmed
         with the *Holy Spirit*.
         What difference do they believe the Holy Spirit
         should make in their lives?   5
     (d)   Before being confirmed young people usually attend
         Confirmation Classes. How important do you think it is
         that candidates are prepared for Confirmation in this way?   5

Although the examination systems of England and Scotland are quite
different, both formats could be used to advantage by teachers within the
teaching process. I have already suggested how tests containing questions at
different levels of difficulty might form part of a number of tasks for
summative or formative purposes. Similarly, teachers in England might find
helpful an approach which makes use of differentiated tests with questions
tied to specific levels of criteria. These would encourage their students to give
of their best since only by completing the task set would they be able to
demonstrate that level of attainment represented by the questions. Although
assessment would most frequently involve differentiation by outcome, this
alternative way of differentiating would constitute a useful check on students'
actual levels of performance.

NOTES AND BIBLIOGRAPHY

1   Michael Hinton *Comprehensive Schools: A Christian's View* SCM 1979,   p96.
2   Scottish Education Department, 'Learning and Teaching in Religious Education', HMSO, 1986.
3   Standard Grade Review of Assessment Group Report, Assessment in Standard Grade Courses, SED, 1986, para.2.17
4   National Curriculum, Task Group on Assessment and Testing, A Report, DES, 1988, para.27
5   Derek Rowntree *Assessing students - How shall we know them?* Harper and Row, 1977, p123
6   Scottish Education Department, 'Assessment for All', 1977.
7   Scottish Education Department, 'Assessment in Standard Grade Courses, 1986', para.3.23.
8   Scottish Education Department, '16-18's in Scotland, Guidelines on Assessment'.
9   'Issues in the Assessment of Affective Characteristics', in *New Developments   in Educational Assessment* ed. H.D. Black and W.B. Dockrell, Scottish Academic Press, 1988, pp137-138.
10   ibid p135
11   E. Clough, P. Davis, R. Summer *Assessing Pupils: A Study of Policy and   Practice* NFER-Nelson, 1984, p8.

12   Religious Education Department, Montrose Academy, Montrose.
13   Quoted in H.Black, 'Assessment for Learning', in *Assessing Educational Achievement* ed. Desmond Nuttall, 1986, p7.
14   See discussion of Bloom in chapter 2.
15   op cit Black, p13.
16   Scottish Education Department, 'Assessment for All', 1977.
17   H.Black and P.Broadfoot *Keeping Track of Teaching* Routledge and Kegan Paul, 1982, p54ff
18   The example is taken from *Attainment in RE: A Handbook for teachers*, Regional RE Centre, Westhill College, Birmingham, 1989
19   see section on 'Failing to Learn', in chapter 2.
20   M. Simpson and B. Arnold, 'Diagnosis in Action', Occasional Paper No.1, Northern College, Aberdeen Campus, 1984,p24
21   H. Black and B. Dockrell, 'Criterion Referenced Assessment in the Classroom', SCRE, 1984, pp151,152.
22   For a fuller discussion of this point see H. Black and M. C. Devine, 'Assessment Purposes: A Study of the Relationship between Diagnostic Assessment and Summative Assessment for Certification', SCRE, 1986.

8 PLANNING COURSES

*Examines different models which have been put forward for planning a
curriculum and sets out a number of principles essential for effective
planning. The thinking behind the introduction of short courses or modules
is explained and a possible structure for a short course descriptor is given,
together with an example. The nature and importance of issues is discussed
and several suggestions are made for planning activities in this area. An
example is provided, involving reasons for and against belief in God.*

WHAT KIND OF PLANNING?

Most teachers are familiar with an approach to planning their teaching which
puts the emphasis on first determining aims and objectives. In a survey of
Scottish schools, HM Inspectorate found that despite the dominance of the
'aims and objectives' approach in curriculum development there were few
signs that individual teachers were planning their courses accordingly.[1] It is
all too easy, it would seem, to take the established content of syllabuses,
particularly those relating to national examinations, as having set our
objectives for us. The teacher's task becomes one of organising suitable
learning experiences to enable students to cover the content. Assessment
concentrates on measuring the extent to which students have grasped this
content, usually by means of an examination similar to the one which will be
set at the end of the course by the examination board. We should not be
surprised if similar practices push their way also into non-examination
courses lower down the school. Of course what students learn through
teaching of this sort may well be extensive as well as valuable. We have no
way of judging. What we need to know is whether what we wish to be
learned is in fact being learned. As we saw in the last chapter, this requires
the establishment of more short term goals and a commitment to assessment
as a necessary part of learning.

In religious education the traditional notion of an agreed syllabus as a list of
content to be taught has long since passed. It has given way to the view that
the first priority is to set out fundamental aims and objectives. Specifying
content is less crucial because different content can be employed to achieve
similar objectives. The trend was started by Avon and Hampshire and
continued by most of the authorities which produced agreed syllabuses in the
eighties. Many of them reflect the work done on objectives by the Schools
Council's Groundplan for the Study of Religion.[2] In Scotland too, no attempt

has been made to prescribe the content of religious education for all schools. Instead, aims, objectives and principles of procedure have been set out so that schools can devise their own courses in accord with their particular religious, social and cultural situation.

Product v Process

One of the earliest models of curriculum planning and one which has been extremely influential throughout the last forty years, is that of Ralph Tyler. Tyler suggested that when planning a curriculum at least four questions need to be answered:

1 What educational purposes should the school seek to attain?
2 What educational experiences can be provided that are likely to attain these purposes?
3 How can these educational experiences be effectively organised?
4 How can we determine whether these purposes are being attained?[3]

This analysis leads to an approach to planning which tries to relate together objectives, content and methodology. It requires us to specify objectives, select appropriate content and methods which will achieve these objectives, and finally to measure how successful we have been.

Much of the criticism relating to such a model has been levelled at the practice of specifying objectives in advance. It is argued that pre-specifying student responses will give the impression that knowledge is static and closed with little or no room for innovation and creativity. The model implies a view of human nature which many people find unacceptable. This is because it regards it as legitimate to determine what students should and should not know, or at least to determine what is most important to learn; and it ignores or fails to take account of students' legitimate interests and desires as well as their right to be treated as free agents responsible for their own destiny. In addition, it is said, such an approach fails to acknowledge the real nature of subject disciplines, most of which contain areas of controversy and debate. In such areas where no right answer is available and where resolutions are a matter of opinion supported by conflicting evidence, to pre-specify learning outcomes in advance amounts to little more than indoctrination.

In contrast to this product or output model others have put forward an alternative process model. The basis of the process model is that teachers and students ought to become involved in worthwhile educational activities rather than be concerned about reaching pre-specified conclusions or acquiring certain information. Teachers and students might be engaged, for example, in developing an understanding of religion through observation, investigation and reflection, as well as in activities such as exploring issues, encouraging critical thinking, and developing a respect for others. The teacher's role is to devise suitable learning experiences which will allow the development of these processes rather than to predict the outcomes of students' learning.[4]

Neither the product or the process model, however, seems sufficient on its own as a basis for curriculum planning. Knowledge, facts and information are essential for the development of understanding. It might be extremely useful therefore for teachers to devise a series of short term objectives relating to key areas of knowledge, as a step towards more process orientated activities. On the other hand a curriculum made up entirely of pre-specified objectives would inevitably be a limited and distorted one. Paul Hirst argues that for curriculum planning to be rational it must begin with a consideration of objectives, before selecting appropriate content and deciding on the means by which the objectives are to be achieved. In his view, it is nonsense to regard a series of processes alone as forming a curriculum or part of a curriculum if they are not designed to obtain specified objectives.

"Unless there is some point to planning the activities, some intended, learnable outcome, however vague this might be, there is no such thing as a curriculum."[5]

Learning Activities

Notwithstanding the significance of objectives and content, it is my contention that much more attention needs to be given to learning activities within overall planning than has previously been the case. We have already noted the persistence in many classrooms of a rather restricted range of teaching approaches making it difficult for many students to learn as effectively as they might otherwise do. As teachers, it seems, we still talk too much! We now know enough about the process of learning to enable us to draw some helpful conclusions. We realise, for example, the importance of starting with what students already know, and of providing sufficient opportunities for revising and reinforcing initial learning. We understand the different ways in which people learn and the need to organise learning so that it is directed at all students and not just the more able. We can see the sense in improving our ability to differentiate within the classroom and the potential contribution to learning which exists through the application of formative assessment. All this points strongly to the crucial part played by learning activities in relation to given content and aims. I would suggest that teachers should set out, even if in note form, detailed descriptions of these learning activities. In this way we can take account of both variety and pace. The following principles are important for adequate planning:

1 Start from what students already know or can do.
2 Use a variety of resources to ensure that learning is accessible to all.
3 Vary teaching approaches to suit the different ways in which people learn.
4 Organise content so that learning concentrates on key ideas and skills.

5   Provide sufficient opportunities for students to reorganise and revise existing knowledge.
6   Determine points at which key aspects of formative and/or summative assessments are to be made.

Let us say, for example, that we want to teach a section on the concept of 'Resurrection' with 13 - 15 year olds:

- First, we need to identify appropriate objectives or learning outcomes which will contribute to the long term goals of the whole course or stage of schooling. This will involve not only product objectives, but also process orientated objectives which have much to contribute to the ability to evaluate, as well as to aspects of the affective domain. Learning outcomes should be wide enough to allow learning to take place across a whole range of different abilities. A learning outcome which requires, for example, the weighing up of alternative viewpoints and the drawing of conclusions will be too difficult for most students to achieve, at least in the time allowed for a particular section.
- Second, we need to select a suitable context within which students can develop their understanding of the concept. In the case of resurrection this might be the stories from Luke's gospel as well as an example of the communion service in one Christian tradition. Also, if students are to make judgements on issues arising from the concept, they will need to know something of the different ways in which Christians view Jesus' resurrection.
- Third, we need to decide on a variety of learning experiences in order to actively involve students with the above content. Reading, writing, listening, watching and talking will all have their place.
- Finally, we need to make available sufficient resources of a kind that will enable all students to handle the content and achieve the learning outcomes to the best of their abilities. The following is an example of what I have come to call a 'summary chart'. It is designed to highlight the importance of planning activities carefully. I have described these activities here in more detail than would be necessary for a teacher's own use.

Learning Activities	Content
Students begin by reading two stories which show the triumph of life over death. In groups of four or five they discuss these for about 15 minutes. They are asked to identify what they regard as special about the stories, and why they are often described as 'resurrection' stories. At the end of the discussion each student writes down his or her own provisional definition of resurrection.	key concept 'Resurrection'; Luke, chapter 24; different interpretations; communion services in two Christian traditions.
Students read or listen to the story of the women finding the empty tomb, before completing a worksheet which draws attention to the miraculous elements and the reactions of the women. Students then find out and explain two ways in which the story is understood by Christians. A class discussion follows on what they have discovered.	**Learning Outcomes** Give a brief definition of the key concept. Explain at least two ways in which Christians understand the resurrection stories. Explain how the communion service expresses Christian belief in resurrection. Express and justify an opinion on issues arising from the concept and the practice.
Students read or listen to the story of the appearances on the road to Emmaus and to the disciples. In groups they explore the meaning of the stories, concentrating on the reactions of the people involved, the statements of Jesus and the intentions of the author. Each group reports its conclusions to the whole class. Having been directed to a number of sources, they identify and explain two ways in which Christians today understand the resurrection stories. A class discussion follows in which the Christian interpretations are compared with the groups' conclusions.	
Students look at slides and/or watch a video showing a communion service in two Christian traditions. They are asked to take notes in which they identify how the services express the meaning of resurrection. Students check their versions against those in selected books, making amendments where necessary. In groups, students identify similarities and differences in belief and practice associated with the communion services of the two traditions, and discuss whether they consider them to be important both for the individual and the whole Christian community. Each group reports its conclusions to the whole class.	**Resources** Stories in 'According to Luke' by Clare Richards, p71f; Church of Scotland, Video; Exploring the Mass, filmstrip, Mayhew McCrimmon; Communion, The Slide Centre; *Search: The Christian Experience*, Gray and McFarlan; *The Many Paths of Christianity* Jan and Mel Thompson; *Christianity: An Approach for GCSE* Kevin O'Donnell.
In groups of four or five, students discuss the question, 'Did Jesus really rise from the dead?' Each group should appoint someone to note down the main points, and time should be given after the discussion for the group to pull together the results. The teacher should be on hand to remind students of certain resources or alternative arguments they might consider. One group should be asked to present its findings to the whole class. This should be followed by a general class discussion in which members of other groups ask questions and make their own comments. Students should then be asked to write their own personal report on,'Did Jesus really rise from the dead?'	*Investigating Jesus* K.R. Chappell; *The Gospel Story of Jesus* Jan Thompson.

Summary charts should be manageable particularly in terms of the amount of content they contain. The tendency to claim that students must know this or that bit of knowledge is a strong one and needs to be resisted. If the course is organised around key concepts and skills, this will help to limit the content by providing a basis for appropriate selection. Having written a first draft of a summary chart, it is worthwhile checking the content again to judge whether or not it is realistic in terms of the time available. The time taken to complete a given set of activities should not be so long that students lose track of the objectives and fail to gain any short term satisfaction or achievement. Nor should it be so short that there is little scope for adequate reinforcement and assessment due to a rush to cover the content. An appropriate time span is probably about eight to twelve hours.

The adequacy of any particular summary chart might be tested using the following questions:
1 Does the content relate to a relevant key concept or skill?
2 Does each learning outcome relate to an appropriate long term goal?
3 Is there a variety of teaching approaches to suit the different ways in which students learn?
4 Is there a sufficient variety of resources to support a wide range of student learning?
5 Are the tasks and activities sufficiently open to allow students with different abilities to demonstrate what they know and can do?

PLANNING SHORT COURSES

In July 1987 the Scottish Education Department announced its decision to extend considerably the provision of short courses for the 14-16 year olds.[6] Although the curriculum was to be based mainly on the two year Standard Grade courses, short courses would be used to enrich the curriculum by providing increased choice on how students might achieve a balanced coverage of the essential modes or areas of experience. They were not to be used to replace Standard Grade courses but were to be seen as complementary to these. In modes for which a minimum time allocation of 160 or 200 hours is recommended, then Standard Grade courses over two years would be the usual means of satisfying the mode. In modes where the minimum time recommended is 80 hours over two years, then nationally devised short courses or courses from the school's own programme would be appropriate to satisfy the mode. This would apply in the areas of 'Technological Activities and Applications', 'Creative and Aesthetic Activities', 'Physical Education', and 'Religious and Moral Education'.[7]

In Scotland, nationally devised Short Courses are certificated by the Scottish

Examination Board and written by joint working groups of the Board and the Scottish Consultative Council on the Curriculum. Normally a single short course will require 40 hours of teaching time and be assessed on a pass/ fail basis without any further discrimination. No attempt is made to grade students' performance except at the basic level of deciding whether or not the student has achieved the specified learning outcomes. Differentiation therefore should be in terms of the programme followed, and students should be offered courses matched to their current levels of attainment. Assessment is entirely internal in relation to specified criteria, and standards are checked through the scrutiny of a Moderator appointed by the Board to serve a number of schools in an area. Proponents of short courses argue that they offer young people clear targets which can be achieved in a reasonably short time giving a sense of satisfaction. However, we have seen that careful planning can introduce such advantages even into full two year courses by breaking down long term goals into shorter term learning outcomes. Through the application of formative and summative assessment, results can be fed back to students as an indication of what has been achieved. At present short courses are available or are being developed in Electronics, Health Studies, Creative and Aesthetic Studies, and Religious and Moral Education.

Planning a short course involves first of all preparing a *short course descriptor*. Each descriptor, regardless of subject, shares common subdivisions or sections and is drawn up according to guidelines laid down by the Scottish Examination Board. The first section sets out the preferred entry level for the course. The short courses in Religious and Moral Education have no specific entry requirement except that students should be beginning at least their third year of secondary education. This would be the fourth year of secondary education in England. Six courses have been developed. They are: A World of Values, Living in a Plural Society, Christianity Today, Investigating a Religion, Moral Issues in Technology, Issues of Belief.[8]

The second main section establishes the purpose and aims of the course. This section should be of such a length that users of the course are left in no doubt as to its intention. The purpose should be stated in terms of general changes which are to be brought about in the learner rather than specific demands, for example: "to provide students with opportunities to acquire knowledge and understanding of some of the basic beliefs of Christianity and how they are practised in a contemporary setting", rather than "explain the meaning of Kingdom of God". Stated in this way the aims of the course should provide a ready basis for working out the learning outcomes.

The third section on learning outcomes is the most central since it is mastery of these that will determine success or failure. The learning outcomes must state clearly what a student should be able to demonstrate as a result of his or her learning. For example, "students should know and understand religious practices within the main Christian traditions". It is recommended that three or four learning outcomes will be sufficient for each 40 hour course and that they should cover all the essential skills and abilities which the course is designed to produce. In Religious and Moral Education this will cover outcomes relating to understanding and evaluation as well as perhaps skills of investigating. The problem with learning outcomes is that they can be ambiguous and open to a wide range of interpretations. In the example above it is not clear precisely what is meant by 'practices', 'main Christian traditions' or 'understanding'.

The fourth and fifth and sixth sections are designed to eliminate as far as possible such ambiguities. The content section sets out appropriate contexts for the learning outcomes. In some cases it will be necessary to set out the content more prescriptively than in others. For example, in the short course entitled, 'Moral Issues in Technology", the learning outcomes for the course are that students should be able to:

1 Identify some examples of developments in technology and explain the advantages and any disadvantages resulting from their use.
2 Demonstrate how the effects of technological developments raise religious/moral questions in two of the following areas: work, the environment and medicine.
3 Complete an investigation into the remaining issue.[9]

The limits of appropriate content here are not difficult to establish. Examples are to be chosen from the specified areas of 'work', the 'environment' and 'medicine', and the content section provides a range of these within each area. On the other hand, the Short Course 'Investigating a Religion' has few limits other than the learning outcomes which are designed to apply to a wide range of differing content. This particular short course is intended to provide an opportunity for students to study a religion of their choice other than Christianity. This can include one of the major world religions or an example of a living primal religion. Although the school's course must be organised around key concepts and related practices, teachers are free to make their own selection of these. The learning outcomes for this course are as follows:

1 Know and understand specified key concepts and evaluate one of these within the religion selected.
2 Know and understand current practices and evaluate one of these within the religion selected.
3 Know and understand the importance of the family and evaluate related issues within the religion selected.[10]

The fifth section attempts to give some advice on learning and teaching approaches. For example, in relation to learning outcome '2' above of the 'Investigating a Religion' Short Course, the following is included: "Activities directed towards the understanding of practices should make use of as much visual material as possible. Pupils should be encouraged to make their own notes on the main features and to discuss these with a partner or in groups. Discussion and research should focus on the purposes of the practice, its significance for the believer, and how successfully it expresses the meaning of one or more of the key concepts. Groups should be given the opportunity to come together in order to share their ideas on this as well as record them in writing. This process should help pupils to begin to identify issues arising from the observance of such practices, and to consider their relevance for people today. Work on practices could be taken together as a discrete section, or each practice could be studied alongside related concepts and sources."[11]

The final section concerns the performance criteria which are associated with each learning outcome. Arguably this is the most important section of all, at least in terms of valid assessment. The performance criteria specify, as unambiguously as possible, those aspects of a learning outcome which demonstrate that the learning outcome has been achieved. In other words the performance criteria set the standard of the learning outcome. Performance criteria should derive logically from the associated learning outcomes. Take the following example:

For a learning outcome such as 'The student evaluates the religious and/or moral dimension of a contemporary environmental issue' a performance criteria such as 'identifies a contemporary environmental issue' would not be relevant. Obviously before embarking on any evaluation of an issue, one would need to have identified it, but such a performance criteria would not furnish any evidence that the student could 'evaluate' as opposed to 'understand' the nature of an environmental issue. The performance criteria must clearly reflect the nature of the learning required by the stated learning outcome. In the 'Investigating a Religion' Short Course the learning outcomes all have three performance criteria associated with them. They are:

Learning Outcome 1: The student
- gives a simple explanation of the key concepts;
- identifies or states significant facts within sources relating to these key concepts;
- expresses an opinion on an issue arising from one of these key concepts or its related sources, supported by at least two valid reasons.

Learning Outcome 2: the student
- identifies or states the main features of selected practices;
- explains in each case how the example of current practice expresses the meaning of the key concept;

- expresses an opinion on an issue arising from one of these practices supported by at least two valid reasons.

Learning Outcome 3: the student
- identifies or states the general moral values and principles which relate to the family;
- explains the viewpoints of the religion on two issues within the family;
- expresses an opinion on one issue within the family supported by at least two valid reasons;[12]

Although the principles outlined here for the design of these courses derive from a national initiative, they are readily transferable to school-based programmes. Teachers could use them in the preparation of courses of a similar length to those described here. Or alternatively, longer courses could be sub-divided into short units. The most important of these principles are:

1 establishing a small number of learning outcomes relating to knowledge, understanding and evaluation.
2 determining several performance criteria for each learning outcome which will show that students have achieved that learning outcome.
3 being clear in advance about the learning activities appropriate to each learning outcome.

We have already noted that short courses are assessed on a pass/fail basis and that no other form of differentiation is applied. It is doubtful whether a period of forty hours is long enough within which to determine levels of attainment for certification beyond a simple pass or fail. Students' performances vary over time and between different topics. Decisions about students' grades should be made on the basis of evidence collected over a longer period and covering a variety of contexts. One of the disadvantages of a pass/fail system is that the principle of 'certification for all', so integral to the reforms within both Standard Grade and GCSE, becomes difficult to maintain. If learning outcomes are set at too high a level then many students will be unable to overtake them within the time limit of 40 hours and so will fail. In theory, of course, this should not happen since students should undertake courses which match their present levels of attainment and stock of abilities. This, however, requires the availability of a wide range of courses, something which is difficult to achieve and justify within just one subject area. If on the other hand the learning outcomes are set too low then many students will pass the course but not receive a certificate which truly reflects their actual attainment.

There is the added problem here of ensuring that such students are able to continue their learning beyond the achievement of basic learning outcomes. Whether they will in practice be enjoined with sufficient motivation so to do is difficult to predict in advance for all courses. The most that any teacher can do is to provide interesting and challenging learning experiences to meet a range of student abilities. This will probably mean among other things supplementing student activities with a range of differentiated tasks along the lines suggested in chapter three. If teachers pay attention to such difficulties and are given adequate support to deal with them, both able and less able students will gain considerable satisfaction from such courses.

TEACHING ISSUES

Alan Watkins, of the Observer, once commented on what he called the stroke of good luck which had overtaken Mr. Michael Heseltine. According to Watkins, Mr. Heseltine had discovered an 'issue'. It was Europe. He continued:

"To an ambitious but disaffected politician, an issue is as an idea to a writer, a concept to a philosopher, or a hypothesis to a scientist. All of a sudden, the way ahead is clear."[13]

To the educator, however, things are hardly so straightforward. To the educator, and even more so to his students, the way ahead becomes muddy, beset with adversity, once an issue has been identified and its challenge addressed. What do others think? How can I find out what they think? What do I think? Can I suppport my opinion with evidence and argument? To an educator an issue is a question, or several related questions, which do not admit of one single correct answer. Instead there may be a range of possible answers none of which appear to settle the issue in any final sense. Nor can it be settled simply by appealing to the evidence since the evidence, itself is likely to be equivocal. Such evidence, however, will not be irrelevant to any answer we wish to give. Since there is no one correct answer, resolution of the issue is not in the hands of either teacher or student, but both. It is a question of judgement.

It is this which furnishes us with the most important reason for dealing with issues in the classroom. Learning about issues is essentially about learning to make judgements. The teacher therefore cannot teach by instruction, at least not without falling into a form of indoctrination. This raises a question about what should be the role of the teacher. Should he aspire to neutrality, for example, when teaching issues and adopt a strategy of being strictly impartial during discussion? Should she take the role of devil's advocate and represent views which the class or group has not yet considered? Or should they adopt a more committed stance when asked by students for their view? Perhaps at different times and on different issues all three will have their place. Issues are windows into real life since little of any importance in life ever admits of one single correct answer. This is why they are so useful to disaffected politicians. Persuade a significant section of the electorate to take your side on an issue which concerns them and you have the makings of power. In religious education there are two kinds of issues:

1   issues which arise from the nature of a religious tradition;
2   issues which arise from within human experience but which for some are mediated through that tradition..

Within Christianity there are numerous issues which have been hotly debated throughout the last decade, not least of which is the question of whether Christian belief in salvation has implications for social organisation and policy or whether it is purely concerned with the destiny of the individual. The Church's insistence on speaking out on issues of poverty, poor housing and urban deprivation has earned it little except acrimony from some quarters. In his commentary on the speech given by the then Prime Minister to the Church of Scotland General Assembly, Jonathan Raban claims that in contrast to the Church of England's thirty-nine articles of faith, Mrs. Thatcher succeeded in reducing Christianity to three basic articles each one emphasising the word choice. These are the belief in the doctrine of Free-Will, in the divinely created sovereignty of individual conscience, and in the Crucifixion and Redemption as the supreme, exemplary acts of choice. Raban writes:

> "The word choice is hammered into each Article, and by Article 3 the meaning of the Crucifixion itself turns out to be that Christ was exercising His right to choose."[14]

Other issues, too, have been widely debated within Christianity, particularly those relating to a physical or spiritual resurrection, and the literal or metaphorical nature of the language of incarnation. Within Hinduism, students could be asked to discuss issues such as the validity of belief in samsara, the relative difficulties associated with the different paths to moksha, or the relevance of ahimsa to the modern world. Within Islam, students could be given opportunities to talk about issues which arise for Muslim children being brought up in a society regarded by many Muslims as permissive and individualist. The implications for young Muslims of the emphasis on authority within Islam might be discussed, along with the relevance of Qur'anic teaching for today.

Human experience presents us with a range of issues which continually challenge the way we look at ourselves and the world around us. Issues related to the nature and destiny of the human being, his or her place and significance in the universe, good and evil, how we treat each other, the reality of God. This concern for 'ultimate' questions is fundamental to the business of religions and much of their conceptual structure and practices have to do with coming to terms with such issues. In this sense religions act as a filter through which people can interpret, explain and celebrate their human existence. But what about the young people with whom as educators we are most concerned? Many of them, if not most, will profess no religion.

They will have given little, if any thought to issues of good and evil, the nature of humankind or the existence of God. And yet it is likely that there will be some such beliefs at the back of their minds, expressed in the values they pursue, the relationships they form, and the priorities they set up. It is the task of religious education to encourage them to come to a more explicit understanding of these beliefs and to help them to make informed judgements in dialogue with the great religious traditions of the world.

A case study

In the preparation of the Standard Grade Religious Studies course we were concerned with the broad question of what ought we to be doing with students in the 14-16 age group. Two factors were particularly important here. First, courses must be appropriate for all students, not just the top 30%. Second, 'what we ought to be doing' was a skills question as well as a content one. And it was through the study of issues, we believed, that the important skills of investigating and evaluating would be developed. We were anxious also to include aspects of study which would serve to attract customers, who might feel for one reason or another that religion was of no interest or value to them. Here again issues of belief and morality, involving as they do question and problems which affect everyone, not just those who are religious, seemed likely to improve motivation. The evidence which we possessed, that most schools spent a good deal of time in any case looking at issues, seemed to confirm this.

During piloting of the course, however, it was the teaching of issues of belief and morality which provided the context for some of our most difficult problems. Initially there were two main tendencies. First, some teachers felt that they had not involved students in sufficient investigating and gathering of different viewpoints, before asking them to take part in discussion. They were relying on students coming up with viewpoints. Consequently discussion tended to revolve around their mostly uninformed opinions. Teachers complained that discussion did not seem to be leading anywhere and, as a result, opportunities for it fell off dramatically. Second, other teachers felt that they allowed students to spend most of their time collecting information *about* issues, rather than providing opportunities for students to discuss what was *at issue* and express their own opinions. Although students did spend some time in pairs or in groups talking about what they had found out, there was still an urgent need to create structured opportunities for students to discuss, formulate views, record them and report back.

An additional difficulty arose concerning the distinction in practice between knowing and understanding an issue, and evaluating it. What precisely are we expecting students to do, teachers asked, when we ask them to evaluate the 'reasons for and against belief in God'. The problem here was that centuries of theological and philosophical speculation meant that there was very little left to say. Arguments for and against the existence of God had been countered and countered again. Was such a process of argument and counter-argument part of knowledge and understanding and did the counter-arguments represent the reasons against? Or was the very participation in this process the essence of learning to evaluate? If so, teachers argued, all but the most able of students would face insurmountable difficulties. All this was in stark contrast to the world religion units where the content and issues were clearly identifiable. Within Christianity, Hinduism, Islam and Judaism, the content consists of key concepts, sources and practices. Issues arise from a consideration of these aspects of the content. Here the content was the issue.

The solution seemed to lie in appropriate planning. Steps had to be taken to ensure that the content or knowledge and understanding component of the issue was clearly identified. Initial activities would then be directed towards encouraging students to find out what is involved by discovering the facts, identifying principles and values, and explaining different viewpoints. Only when this had been done would students become involved in the process of considering implications and forming judgements. The process might be shown as follows:

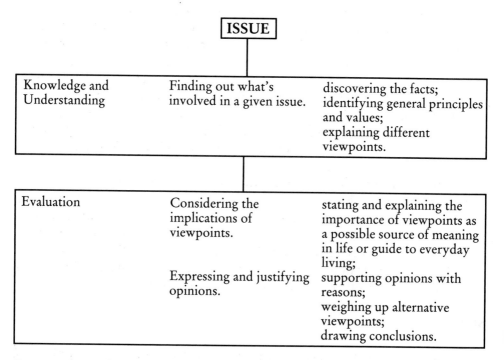

ISSUE		
Knowledge and Understanding	Finding out what's involved in a given issue.	discovering the facts; identifying general principles and values; explaining different viewpoints.
Evaluation	Considering the implications of viewpoints.	stating and explaining the importance of viewpoints as a possible source of meaning in life or guide to everyday living;
	Expressing and justifying opinions.	supporting opinions with reasons; weighing up alternative viewpoints; drawing conclusions.

Reasons for and against belief in God might be selected from nature, morality and religious experience. Students could be set the task of finding out and explaining viewpoints relating to these areas as well as being given opportunities to talk to each other about what they have found out. During this process they will inevitably be reflecting critically on what they are learning, although more structured activities for discussing different viewpoints will be necessary. Students should be encouraged to say what they think about the standard reasons for and against belief in God. As well as explaining specific viewpoints and commenting on them students should also be given opportunities to take a number of different and opposing viewpoints together, present an argument and draw conclusions. In a school I visited regularly, students were asked on one occasion to complete a piece of extended writing on the subject, 'Is God a product of people's imagination?' The following represents two students' work. As we have already noted in chapter six on evaluation, even students in the 13 - 15 age group find it difficult to weigh up alternative viewpoints and draw conclusions. In these examples, Student A seems more advanced in this regard than Student B.

Student A

"In this essay I will discuss whether or not God is a product of people's imagination. Everybody has different ideas about this question, there are many arguments for and against. Firstly has anybody ever seen God or heard him? Some people say they have had religious experiences eg. they say during a short loss of life in an operating theatre that they have seen God or even spoke to him. People who are against this say that people make up God as soon as any problems arise in their lives. As the psychologist Freud said, 'People invent God in times of need.' There are many examples of religious experience in the Bible where people have spoken to God. God spoke to Moses for example through a burning bush. But no one can know this for a fact. It might have been just a story made up and passed down from generation to generation. Who knows?

"If there is no God then where did the world come from, where did we come from. Everything must have a beginning and come from somewhere. If you are a believer you would say that God is the cause of it all. If you are not you would say that we don't need a creator to explain the world, we don't need to say the world had a beginning. If everything was made by God who made him? These are some of the things you should take into account when deciding whether you believe in God."

Student B

"In this essay I will discuss whether or not God is a product of people's imagination. Firstly I will look at what some people have said about the question. Yuri Gagarin said, 'I travelled through space, but I did not see

God'. This quote from Yuri probably means that he thought people believed in a God who lived up in the clouds. So when he travelled through space he looked for him but could not see him. In addition to what Yuri Gagarin said, Freud a psychologist said that 'People invent God in times of need'. This means that when people are in trouble they turn to God or as Freud said they invent God.

"Some people, however, believe that God is the power or spirit which created the world and is still available to people today. People do not invent him he is real. For evidence they point to the changes that have taken place in some people's lives. Nicky Cruz was a very violent person whose life was completely changed. He believes that God spoke to him and came into his life proving that someone, that is God, did care about him. This is an example of religious experience which many people say they have had."

Below I have set out reasons for and against belief in God which would constitute the basis of the knowledge and understanding component of this issue. I have also included in italics examples of what might be said by way of critical comment.

Reasons For

• Nature
Every event has its explanation in previous events, which in turn refer to even earlier events. Every event within the universe has been caused by earlier events. The same must be true of the universe itself. It too must have a cause. Someone or something must have created it. And that creator must itself be uncreated and uncaused by anything else. It was the First Cause.
But why should we not take the physical universe to be the ultimate unexplained reality. The universe itself may be a succession of events which as a whole is uncaused and not dependent on anything beyond itself.

• Morality
I am conscious that I should try to do what is right and avoid what is evil. This moral obligation to do good must come from a source outside myself and must itself be good. This source we call God.
But moral obligation arises from the fact that we are basically social by nature. In order to live in community we have had to develop rules. These rules are seen as obligations because they are necessary for the survival and flourishing of any society.

• Religious experience
Religious experience, whether shared by a number of people of public events

or purely private, reflecting some inner religious encounter or enlightenment is most naturally explained as a manifestation of the divine.

But there are other causes of such experiences apart from the activity of a transcendent God. There are hallucinatory visions, voices, senses of presence, experienced by people who are insane as well as those in deep emotional states of grief or longing.

Reasons Against

• Nature

There is no need for a God because everything in the world, including religion, can be adequately explained without it. Religion is merely the creation of the human mind designed to provide us with some comfort amidst the harsh realities of life.

But this does not mean that the claims made by religion about God and the world are false. The fact that religion is presented as good news for people in despair does not show that it is not true. In any case religion does not always offer comfort. It also offers challenge, personal sacrifice, and a sometimes unwanted demand to face up to our responsibilities.

• Morality

There is no God because no God of love would allow the degree of pain and suffering which exists in the world. There is first of all a range of bodily sufferings which affects millions of people every day, due to disease, hunger, blindness, brain damage and other forms of disablement. In addition there is emotional suffering due to bereavement, loneliness, fear, remorse, and hatred.

But the world as we know it is a world within which human beings grow and develop in response to challenges and problems. There is failure as well as success, disaster as well as triumph. A world in which all pain and suffering has been eliminated and in which there were therefore no problems to be solved or challenges to be met, would not be an environment in which human beings could strive towards growth and maturity.

Notes and Bibliography

1   Scottish Education Department, 'Learning and Teaching in Scottish Secondary Schools: The Contribution of Educational Technology', 1982, para 1.6
2   Schools Council, 'A Groundplan for the Study of Religion', 1977
3   A.V. Kelly *The Curriculum: Theory and Practice* Harper and Row, 1982, p11
4   Denis Lawton *Curriculum Studies and Educational Planning* Hodder & Stoughton, p108
5   Paul Hirst, 'Philosophy and Curriculum Planning', in *Knowledge and the Curriculum* Routledge and Kegan Paul, 1974, p3
6   Scottish Education Department, Circular 1157
7   Scottish Consultative Council on the Curriculum, Guidelines for Headteachers, 1989, Appedix F
8   see Scottish Examination Board, Joint Working Group Report on Moral, Social and Religious Education, Short Courses, 1990
9/12   ibid SEB
13   Alan Watkins *The Observer* 21 May 1989
14   Jonathan Raban *God, Man and Mrs. Thatcher: Counterblasts No.1* Chatto, 1989, p33
15   I am grateful to Mrs Roseleen Thorne, former Head of the RE Department at Linksfield Academy for permission to use these examples of students' work.

INDEX